Stop Being Nice

Stop Overthinking and Live a Happy Life

(Step by Step Guide on How to Stop Being Arrogant So as to Build Healthy)

Marcus Gammage

Published By **Chris David**

Marcus Gammage

All Rights Reserved

Stop Being Nice: Stop Overthinking and Live a Happy Life (Step by Step Guide on How to Stop Being Arrogant So as to Build Healthy)

ISBN 978-0-9953115-9-6

No part of this guidebook shall be reproduced in any form without permission in writing from the publisher except in the case of brief quotations embodied in critical articles or reviews.

Legal & Disclaimer

The information contained in this book is not designed to replace or take the place of any form of medicine or professional medical advice. The information in this book has been provided for educational & entertainment purposes only.

The information contained in this book has been compiled from sources deemed reliable, and it is accurate to the best of the Author's knowledge; however, the Author cannot guarantee its accuracy and validity and cannot be held liable for any errors or omissions. Changes are periodically made to this book. You must consult your doctor or get professional medical advice before using any of the suggested remedies, techniques, or information in this book.

Upon using the information contained in this book, you agree to hold harmless the Author from and against any damages, costs, and expenses, including any legal fees potentially resulting from the application of any of the information provided by this guide. This disclaimer applies to any damages or injury caused by the use and application, whether directly or indirectly, of any advice or information presented, whether for breach of contract, tort, negligence, personal injury, criminal intent, or under any other cause of action.

You agree to accept all risks of using the information presented inside this book. You need to consult a professional medical practitioner in order to ensure you are both able and healthy enough to participate in this program.

Table Of Contents

Chapter 1: Craving Approval 1

Chapter 2: Raising People Pleasers 16

Chapter 3: People Pleasing At Home...... 25

Chapter 4: Innerfearfreaks..................... 29

Chapter 5: Family 41

Chapter 6: Father Relationship 53

Chapter 7: Parenting.............................. 61

Chapter 8: Friendships 68

Chapter 9: Intimate Relationships.......... 74

Chapter 10: Love, Sex And Sexuality 83

Chapter 11: Women Misogynists 98

Chapter 12: The Post-Metoo Workplace 103

Chapter 13: The Five Superpowers 128

Chapter 14: Psychology Of Assertiveness 151

Chapter 1: Craving Approval

Let's communicate about THAT character. You understand the high-quality – the famous man/female at college, the high-quality sharp fashionable mamma you have got got met at a little one group, the cool AF on-line influencer you observe. THAT character. You want them to like you lots. Because in a few manner being preferred with the beneficial resource of the 'cool baby' validates your very existence.

I don't want to remember how an lousy lot of my energy, creativity and ingenuity I used up seeking to please that man or woman at special elements in my existence. From what I wore spherical them to constructing some thing witty to mention – I craved their approval so much. In my mind, they have been without a doubt plenty higher than me; within the occasion that they appreciated me then via a few way I might be a better person. This is a few component that is pretty clean to permit flow into of as you begin ditching your people pleaser. As you value your self extra you begin to like yourself more. When you need and apprehend yourself, the want to electrify humans you don't recognize begins offevolved to diminish. Remember, you've got all the tools within the course of this e-book to guide your non-public adventure.

In real life and on social media, there are layers and layers of this humans-captivating detail. I've been caught up in what I modified into posting on social media due to the reality I desired the those who I observe - the cool kids - to approve of what I turn out to be writing.

I favored validation from people whose critiques remember to me. When I realised that I even have come to be doing this, I checked myself. While I can appreciate those people, their returning the admiration doesn't in truth make a difference to me and my charge in the international.

There is an episode of Black Mirror referred to as Nosedive. In it, the protagonist is so determined for scores on social media that her lifestyles is going from superb sanitised pastel-coloured perfection to a grubby mess. Why? Because she didn't get the approval that she so desperately sought which took its toll. While social media has brought approximately many benefits, we can not deny the psychosocial effect of such systems and the need for 'likes' and validation. Social media can increase your people pleaser.

When we look at how important our formative relationships are, it makes feel that we crave approval from others. If we're no longer widespread, then with the resource of default we're rejected, which is going towards our survival instincts. Early stories approximately what being selfish is and the way you want to be extremely good don't dIsappear while you emerge as an individual. But, as adults, our validation can now not be sustained via extraordinary peoples' approval. We are not relying on others – or their approval people – to live on. Our survival instincts, however, didn't get this memo – they're regardless of the truth that brought about via using rejection. External validation is fleeting and transient. Self-compassion and self-apprehend are everlasting and are what is needed to shift inside the course of self-popularity.

When I first started out out speakme approximately people fascinating it have end up without a doubt interesting to hear and feature a have a look at some of the remarks. I heard from some humans announcing that they did now not want to be egocentric via using putting themselves first. Some were angry, insisting they needed to people please, like there was no excellent opportunity and this changed into what made you a 'appropriate' human. This notion is deeply ingrained.

So, allow us to have a have a study the biological/evolutionary want to be traditional and what you need to revel in steady and cherished. Thousands of years ago, while we lived in smaller 'tribal' groups, rejection from the circle of relatives organization might have induced death – either via hungry sabre-toothed tigers, or extraordinary clans. Our primitive ('reptilian') thoughts managed our automated self-preserving behaviours to ensure our survival. Anything that turned into a hazard to our safety (survival) might have inspired our amygdala and alerted our sympathetic traumatic machine, flooding our body with adrenaline and cortisol and triggering the combat-flight-freeze reaction; this have come to be sufficient to prevent us performing some component that risked rejection from the community.

We have evolved in how we stay our lives however we no matter the fact which have our primitive thoughts. Our surroundings may also additionally have modified and we might not be faced with the equal threats as our ancestors, but we're nevertheless met with in all likelihood risky conditions. When we feel threatened (or recognize that we're under chance), the same survival response is brought approximately. Someone not accepting you could stimulate your amygdala, which sends a message for your sympathetic concerned machine, and because of this the equal inner response is created. It's this response that we then end up reactive to, manifesting as seemingly irrational or negative behaviours. Understanding that is crucial to knowledge why sure conditions purpose you.

Maslow's Hierarchy of Needs

You is probably familiar with Maslow's hierarchy of dreams which state the order of human desires:

1. Physiological
2. Safety

3. Belonging and Love

four. Esteem

5. Self-Actualization

'Physiological' and 'safety' are your most primary dreams for survival and include meals and shelter (and, in a capitalist society, the coins to pay for them). Belonging, love and esteem are classed as your emotional desires, and self-actualisation is taken into consideration your self-fulfilment (growth) want. Generally, people want to fulfill decrease degree dreams earlier than moving directly to the following degree. If someone is residing hand-to-mouth every month and suffering to fulfill the most number one needs of food and safe haven, then love and belonging might not be a difficulty.

People charming can effect our needs being met and wherein we take a seat constant with Maslow's hierarchy. When we're looking for approval and prioritise meeting the needs of others (on the fee of our private), we stay stuck at the bottom of the hierarchy. This can appear to be tolerating hurtful and abusive behaviours and now not 'rocking the boat' to make certain our dreams for protection are met. When we're searching for love and belonging, we might also human beings please to make certain that those dreams are met, believing that stunning others is the exceptional way to sense loved and benefit a experience of belonging. It's smooth to look how, at the equal time as we are caught in a cycle of humans-lovely, our self-actualisation (increase) is limited, or seemingly now not possible.

On the flipside, even as we prioritise (and take responsibility for) our non-public desires over others, and discover ways to esteem ourselves from the inner (in preference to relying on outdoor validation), we're able to see how growth turns into possible. Now, this isn't to say that once you bought self-actualisation you'll in no way drop returned to the bottom of the hierarchy (physiological and protection) – such is the ambiguity that we can be developing AND locate ourselves living in survival mode. We've in reality visible this with the global pandemic as human beings lost their jobs and earnings and needed to re-prioritise their most number one of dreams. However, we are able to absolutely see how human beings-alluring stunts our boom and forestalls us from undertaking our whole ability in all elements of our lives.

Before I pass on I want to make a easy difference among human beings-applicable and cooperation, and this is specifically important to understand when you have (or art work with) youngsters. I've often heard humans reward kids who want to satisfaction others as even though it's a actually effective detail. Let me inform you now: it's not. We do now not want to raise human beings pleasers. So masses of us are experiencing mental issues as adults due to human beings perfect as children.

Of route, we want our youngsters to cooperate and to be kind. Firstly, there is a large distinction among being 'superb' and being type. Niceness comes from the pinnacle (ego); kindness comes from the coronary coronary heart. If you've ever expert any shape of emotional abuse, you'll realize that the maximum abusive and narcissistic of human beings (I'm speaking tendencies, not illness right right right here) additionally can be the most fascinating to the outdoor worldwide. Equally, as people pleasers, our want to be splendid comes from our egoic want for approval.

Cooperation, and analyzing to get alongside in a society with exceptional human beings, is a survival method (as mentioned earlier). This studying happens as a herbal a part of the socialisation system (albeit loads socialisation nowadays is pressured and takes area in very artificial environments, e.G. Many mainstream faculties). And at the same time as cooperation sounds very similar to human beings charming, it's certainly approximately being an same member of society. It's about making sure everybody's needs are met. Egalitarian societies - as an instance, hunter-gatherer businesses - require cooperation because of the reality every person is identical and all assets are shared equally. People charming, however, follows a particular dynamic. It's approximately power and manipulate, the human beings pleaser basically taking the function of the 'victim' or, extra generally, the 'martyr'. For people alluring to art work as a dynamic, there needs to be a person assuming control and taking the 'perpetrator' position; there aren't any equals.

So, as parents (or absolutely everyone who works with kids in any capability), whilst we approve of our infant's 'want to thrill' what we're surely announcing is that this: I approve of you behaving in a manner that makes me more comfortable and is more palatable to me and different adults. And, if we need to head a step in addition, we're announcing: you are making me look like a better discern (teacher/care employee and so forth.) i.E. You make me look like I'm on top of things (hidden inference: of myself). As maximum folks do not live in egalitarian societies, it's honest to assume that children are typically taken into consideration as 'lesser than' and therefore anticipated to perform in a way this is appropriate (and accessible) to adults.

As a infant, if your goals have been not met through the ones you trusted to meet them, you could probable have made it your responsibility to fulfill theirs. People eye-catching could probably were a survival instinct. If you become aware about as being a people pleaser as a toddler, then it's in all likelihood that your number one goals have been not met. Going again to Maslow's hierarchy of desires, even if you have been fed, clothed and had a roof over your head, you may no longer have moved past your physiological wishes (degree 1). The need to revel in steady (degree 2) requires emotional and non secular safety, now not genuinely physical. While plenty of our parents and ancestors may need to provide for our bodily protection, inside the occasion that they have got been stuck in survival mode and themselves no longer feeling emotionally secure (or suppressed their feelings), they might not had been capable of provide that diploma of safety for us.

Many of us were raised with the aid of the use of emotionally bad adults who projected their trauma and wounds, or had been emotionally unavailable; cyclical patterns that repeat each generation when left unchecked. This would in all likelihood have exacerbated our want to satisfaction those spherical us, bonding us to their ache and developing co-installation determine-baby relationships. Luckily, we've got a bargain greater cognizance of emotional fitness and neuroscience now, and understand the importance of emotional expression in choice to suppression. However, the effects of no longer having our emotional goals met might possibly have imprinted on us and, in masses of times, been carried into adulthood as trauma and Adverse Childhood Experiences (ACEs). (We will have a look at ACEs in financial ruin 6.)

As adults, there are numerous methods to triumph over and heal our early life reports. Through neuroscience and our records of neuroplasticity, we now realise that, as lots as our young human beings memories have formed our mind (and subsequent behaviours, addictions and present day properly being), we are able to create new neural connections and responses and consequently new effects. We can ruin the cycles and study a one-of-a-kind manner of being.

Meditation

Scientists for the time being are beginning to investigate the effects of this ancient workout. First believed to be practiced in India in the Vedic and/or early Hindu colleges, it is idea that Chinese Taoist and Indian Buddhist traditions advanced their non-public versions of meditation practices. Recent research from Harvard University said in the mag Psychiatry Research shows that meditation can alternate the structures of the mind with the aid of the use of increasing the conical thickness in the hippocampus which, alongside unique roles, regulates feelings. If meditation can adjust emotions, it is able to resource us on our direction to getting higher from people desirable.

Chapter 2: Raising People Pleasers

Let me inform you the story of a 'bossy' and precocious infant. Spoiler alert: it's me. Now, this more youthful lady have come to be born, as you have got been, brimming with self notion – absolutely unfastened, expressive, and in contact with every part of herself. She grow to be the primary toddler; a lady who stated what she wanted, felt what she felt, and did what she did. A female who felt deeply and who expressed herself freely. Except, of route, that she become labelled 'too bossy' and 'precocious' thru the adults round her, all within earshot or immediately to her face. It would possibly seem the sector didn't much like assertive younger ladies.

I noticed the injustice in my worldwide. I made signs and signs and symptoms and fundraised and joined charities. I even have grow to be a vegetarian, joined WWF (the flora and fauna charity, not the wrestling federation!), and stood up for what I believed end up proper.

I campaigned in my domestic for my mum to forestall smoking thru plastering 'No Smoking Zone' posters over the car and house. (It paid off two decades later whilst she did in the end stop.)

Old earlier than my time, I became wiser than what changed into expected for someone in their unmarried digits, however greater younger sufficient to be anticipated to blindly recognize the whole lot someone older than me stated. (I discovered out this whilst my mum grow to be referred to as in to talk with my primary school teacher approximately my 'mindset' trouble.) Thus, a constriction regarded for this rather touchy toddler.

Being lots older, I now understand that sensitivity is a gift – a present that includes such pretty a few superpowers. However, while you are eight and also you don't recognize the way to address your emotions (or genuinely anyone else's), whilst you don't understand that you could pick up on anyone's electricity or what having clair sentience method, sensitivity doesn't feel like a gift. When it isn't always nurtured like a gift it rapid will become a burden.

Instead of embracing her sensitivity and seeing it for the present that it modified into (had she realised that honestly it was a gift), 8-three hundred and sixty five days-vintage Kara became wondering, 'All the ones older humans are saying that being a bossy woman is lousy and I were informed I am bossy. They hate me pronouncing what I suppose or not following the road. I had been told again and again that adults are to be listened to and obeyed.' The voices and opinions of others are internalised as disgrace, so we right away discover ways to suppress our 'flaws'.

I made a aware choice to healthy in, to conform, to turn out to be a good deal much less of this and more of that. Though I ought to mention that, regardless of analyzing the manner to healthy in, I however popped out of that subject often – you can't maintain a bossy and precocious teenager down for that long, although society dictates in any other case.

I pay hobby adults say to their youngsters, 'Be quiet at the same time as adults are speakme,' or they're now not listening or being present to their children. No judgement here – it's now not feasible to be gift one hundred% of the time. But we are capable of create a courting based totally mostly on mutual recognize, accept as authentic with and compassion. The antique adage 'kids need to be visible and no longer heard' doesn't in shape with a more respectful technique to toddler-rearing, however, this attitude towards children however remains. We've visible this need to 'quash' the voice and spirit of children and more youthful people show up on a larger scale, the outpouring of bile (considerably with the useful resource of the usage of adults) in the path of the more youthful climate justice activists being the precise example.

How dare they venture our generation?' 'What does a sixteen three hundred and sixty five days antique understand!' 'They need to be in college getting to know no longer protesting.'

This is so dismissive and closed-minded. The misogyny, childism and ridiculousness of humans wondering that, because they may be older, they will be robotically assumed wiser. And now not simplest that but looking for more youthful human beings to suppress who they're to make the adults spherical them sense greater cushty (and normally, superior). You might have take a look at a few greater books, have greater qualifications and life experience, and be the version tax-paying citizen, but this doesn't suggest that you know better. Let more youthful people be. In distinct terms, allow them to unique themselves. Yes, as a guardian, figure, or teacher you have were given a obligation for extra youthful people's welfare – fitness, protection, health, safety - but it is not your location to censor or mould them into variations of what's sanitised and palatable through your requirements. Young people do no longer should learn how to human beings please. They do now not exist to meet your wishes or approval. And if we're talking approximately having a duty for their protection, permit's make sure that we're which incorporates emotional protection too. Learning to ignore your very private emotions and goals, and studying to stuff down emotions, does now not allow one to sense emotionally stable. While this is a survival technique to create the illusion of safety, masses people in the meanwhile are (as adults) having to undo an lousy lot of that conditioning and heal from the traumas and highbrow fitness problems that arose as a end result.

It is essential for all of our recognition and the survival of this planet that our youngsters do no longer repeat this cycle. Surely, one of the motives the planet is in so much hassle is that kids get 'educated' in a manner to match in as teenagers and no longer undertaking the popularity quo?

I actually have 0 preference for my little one to people please. I love how kind and beneficiant he's, and I love that he is additionally his personal character. He has now not been educated in 'a manner to be splendid', however as dad and mom we model admire and kindness and inspire him to undergo in mind his characteristic in the international and society. We communicate about racism, privilege, and society. We moreover inspire his innate kindness and attention, and provide him the gap to be all of who he is. I communicate about gratitude and appreciation with him. We ask him no longer to grab or make needs, on the equal time as knowledge that he is young and gaining knowledge of all of the time. We understand as dad and mom we're going to do it all imperfectly.

Being hyper aware of the recollections around human beings charming, I see it in kids lots, specially women. There is an excessive amount of popularity positioned on whether or not they'll be 'performing' how they need to. Too many girls are knowledgeable 'be terrific' from an early age, then after they hit teens they are knowledgeable it doesn't rely if humans like them or not. By that element, any extraordinary messages are drowned out with the aid of using the usage of the indoctrination of our modern-day-day society.

I would really like to expect Generation Z can growth up thinking humans captivating is not a part of lifestyles, and being exquisite is not a few thing to strive for. Instead, their inner traits of kindness, love and generosity can lead the manner.

If you do no longer need the youngsters in your existence to make bigger up people beautiful, then how are you modelling that? Are you being a people pleaser round them? If you're, it is time to do the work. For your increase, it is vital that you learn how to unpack your human beings lovely testimonies, conduct and behaviours so you can faucet lower back into your inner attention.

To start, you ought to re-discover what your tale is – wherein, while and why you made a decision to human beings please in the first location. Identifying this shows you could located the proverbial finger on it and apprehend yourself (and your behaviours) in a deeper way. That reputation and facts offers you compassion; from compassion comes perception and from belief comes desire – the choice to preserve humans captivating … or not.

Chapter 3: People Pleasing At Home

People proper within the domestic is rife, displaying up because the (often unspoken) expectations of you (and your feature) within the home, collectively with the emotional properly-being of anyone and the each day strolling of the own family. As humans pleasers, we take on the responsibilities, now not wishing to bitch or ask for assist, which often consequences in resentment and strained relationships. Note that humans-attractive within the home could be very masses tied to binary gender stereotypes and expectancies; resentment can brew on every elements.

Who bears the weight of the bulk of the unseen or invisible labour in your house? Aside from the practical duties you do, it's essential that you get easy on what invisible obligations you do additionally. When I wrote my list, it regarded like this:

Help Arthur get prepared earlier than college

Arrange appointments for Arthur – dentist, scientific doctor, homeopath

Keep on pinnacle of the laundry

Make fantastic the cat is healthy

Arrange our excursion plans

Roughly, understand everyone's timetable for each week

Liaise with letting agent concerning the house we are in

Now, my accomplice and I without a doubt have a 50/50 relationship with the practicalities – he does the cooking, is a father to his infant (now not a babysitter, he's taking whole obligation of being a 50/50 caregiver), takes the bins out, and helps with the laundry.

I do now not experience placed upon or resentful in our home lifestyles. I do no longer do cooking or meal making plans, so that may be a big bite of labour taken away.

We percentage cleaning and tidying. My partner takes the initiative and puts matters away, and gets topics performed without me 'nagging'. At the equal time, once I in reality sat with how an lousy lot time and power of mine is used up in the minutia of those invisible duties, I end up surprised.

Recognising this and speaking approximately it's miles key – having that reputation and a time period to define it makes a global of difference. Acknowledging that you have a listing of 'to-dos' and that a huge bite of it's far 'invisible' labour way you can begin studying which of these obligations are appealing you, and which can be attractive others.

If you're doing most of the invisible labour in your house and are feeling envious about it, you then honestly are humans suitable.

Be privy to invisible responsibilities like:

Keeping the peace all the time in the residence

Organising every body else's timetables

Being the only who actually all of us off-loads onto, emotionally

Being the best who buys all of the gifts for all activities

How are you feeling about them? Do you do them due to the fact you like to do them, or because of the reality you enjoy you 'have' to?

Reflection Point: Write out your list – all of the to-dos you do each day together with the invisible labour and unseen movements. Go through that listing and exercising what is sincerely weighing you down. Pick at the least one and discover a way to save you doing it, get aid with it, or start working on a plan to permit it circulate.

Chapter 4: Innerfearfreaks

When you test human beings-lovable to your day by day lifestyles, you need to apprehend the innerFEARfreaks and the manner they effect the strategies you have interaction with the area. If now not whatever else, you can benefit a feel of alleviation for understanding that it's no longer 'genuinely you'. Having facilitated businesses on and offline for over 10 years now, the maximum essential remedy may be felt even as someone hears you assert, 'I experience like this … One of my memories is ….' Every time, there may be someone else inside the room who thinks, 'Holy shit, I feel like that too. I actually have that story.'

As tons as we expect we're by myself and our story is specific, we are an extended manner extra related than we recognise. So insidious is human beings-appealing which you probable have a good buy more commonplace floor with human beings than you watched! It's a chunk like social tension.

We experience annoying in sure social conditions, assuming that the human beings we're mingling with are awesome assured and in control. Yet they too are experiencing social anxiety, themselves carrying a mask of confidence and bravado to cover it. There is lots electricity even as we percent our emotions and studies, giving others permission to drop the mask and create a deeper connection.

This ebook is centered on the human beings pleaser who, for me, has been my dominant innerFEARfreak in lots of situations. However, there are four others which interweave with the people pleaser. Knowing them, expertise them, and operating to combine them are paramount to feeling connection, abundance, pride and peace – whilst they're unacknowledged, they run amok and block the deeper evaluations that come with presence.

The InnerFEARfreaks are really worth in their own ebook. What follows is a summary to help you start this exploratory artwork. (If you'd like to take it similarly, I'll will can help you comprehend how at the surrender of this economic wreck.)

Alongside the people pleaser, the innerFEARfreaks are:

1) The Control Freak

2) The Drama Queen

three) The Perfectionist

4) The Inner Rebel/Unheard Child

The Control Freak

The Control Freak is probably one of the handiest to understand, as the need to control is some element absolutely everyone evaluations in some manner or every extraordinary. Needing to recognize how subjects will pan out, trying a person to act in a amazing way, fear of factors now not going the manner you want, or stressful approximately topics that have lengthy beyond incorrect in advance than are very plenty tied in with our want for fact (and therefore our need for protection, as discussed within the previous financial disaster).

If your manipulate freak is dominant, you'll notice you are clenched and maintaining pretty some tension in your body. You might be absolutely poised to do a little trouble and discover it tough to update off. You might be stage-handling delight but surely leaving very little room for it via spontaneity.

Understanding in which our manipulate dispositions and memories got here from and what they recommend to you'll launch some of that need to govern. The antidote is to keep in mind and surrender – very tough on the equal time as you're a control freak. The reality is, we cannot manage a few element or absolutely everyone out of doors human beings, and in search of to uses up a number of power. Getting comfortable with uncertainty – however a whole lot this is going closer to our conditioning – will will assist you to lean into recall and surrender.

People-captivating is a shape of manipulate, and manage is a form of humans-appealing. What the control freak can offer you with - through understanding, attention and launch of manage - is profound believe and vicinity to allow the unexpected to go back via and the larger plan to unfold.

The Drama Queen

The Drama Queen may be the loudest of all of the innerFEARfreaks. Thriving on subjects going wrong, catastrophising, getting a kick out of being the sufferer – she in no way breaks the victim cycle.

When your drama queen is dominant you may be on your head lots and stuck in an limitless loop of communique, typically about subjects that haven't came about however but make you experience pretty irritated. Ever played an imaginary scenario over and over on your head until you're so labored up ... however now not a few issue has definitely passed off? That's your drama queen! You can also find out your energy is ungrounded and which you react to the entirety.

There can be little or no peace at the same time as your drama queen is dominant. Being capable of unpack the memories and critiques which have created the cycle of harm and sadness will bring about region to be present and to pick out to respond in preference to react. You circulate from a place of reactivity to boundless love and compassion for you and all people spherical you.

The Perfectionist

The Perfectionist is all about the need for things to be truely so (and may be very carefully connected to the Control Freak). Even more than that is the need to meet some impossibly best favored. This might be to do collectively along with your look, body, art work, how you're as a determine, partner or friend – there are a myriad of locations the Perfectionist shows up. There is a lot of resentment locked into the Perfectionist. Understanding in which the proper breed of satisfactory comes from for you manner that you could rein for your internal perfectionist and, as an alternative, enjoy imperfection.

When your inner perfectionist is dominant, you can have an internal talk saying things like:

I want to wait till I get x earlier than I can do that or before I am equipped.'

I need to look like this earlier than I do this.'

I want to apprehend I've have been given this 100 in line with cent right in advance than I begin.'

These mind keep you caught in compete and evaluate, and/or procrastination.

If you pay interest your internal perfectionist as speak on your head, it is important to get clear on whose voice it is. Is it yours or someone else's? Where do you sense tension for your frame at the same time as you feel the need for topics to be 'ideal'?

Your perfectionist often goes hand in hand with the people pleaser, because of this which you set (and strive for) idealistic goals and expectancies, at the identical time as concurrently disconnecting from what you need and want. Even even as you achieve your desires, you in no way feel the way you want to.

By accepting your internal perfectionist, you are proficient the capability to fall deeply in love with yourself and feel elegance on each degree. The antidote is imperfect motion:

without a doubt carry out a touch factor imperfectly, whatever it's miles.

The Inner Rebel/Unheard Child

One of the maximum complex of the innerFEARfreaks is often diagnosed as your internal toddler.

She may come out whilst you enjoy

unstable

unheard

unseen

Any unhealed mom/father wounds (blanketed in extra detail in Section 2) are associated with our inner infant. When you sense in ache, it's a sign that your inner infant dreams some aspect. When you act up, this is often a signal that your inner upward thrust up dreams a few element she is not getting. Your internal little one is fuelled every and each time you supress an emotion or allow clearly one of your goals pass unmet. (Unmet goals = traditional signal of people attractive.)

When you are taking a seat with the Inner Rebel/Unheard Child, she reminds you that YOU want your love, hobby and recognize. Sit with your self and be with a few detail feelings you have got were given. At times while you do make mistakes, don't forget which you are human; lessen out the self-shaming and cope with your self with real compassion.

While the 7-Step Exploration at some point of this book is meant to your humans pleaser, you can additionally use it for each of the opposite innerFEARfreaks while they're walking the show. If there may be fine one element you do whilst analyzing this e-book, make it the 7-Step Exploration (despite the fact that, of course, you'll gain charge from all of the property inner the ones pages).

Using this approach doesn't mean you'll come to be your innerFEARfreak. But you may be completely present to all components of you, and get right of access for your connection for your Higher Self/Intuition/God within the most powerful way. If you do now not renowned your innerFEARfreaks and paintings with them, then you definately are permitting them to run the show from a place of ache, worry and beyond tales. Your functionality to transport deeper and deeper with them on every occasion will carry you once more to the prevailing.

Section 2: People Pleasing ... in Relationships

In this phase we will cover one of the additives of lifestyles that brings us every delight and pain, often in same degree: relationships. From circle of relatives to friendshIps and our maximum intimate of relationships, we crave belonging. As stated inside the previous segment, our need for belonging can often come at the charge of our very non-public happiness and well-being, specially whilst we trade our goals for the ones of others.

We all want to be common, visible, heard, loved and understood, however, a whole lot of the conditioning and ache we take into maturity comes due to not feeling those topics at some point of our childhood and youth. Typically, to make sure our experience of belonging (and survival), we over atone for our unmet goals with the useful resource of overindulging the goals of these in our relationships – conventional people beautiful territory!

Chapter 5: Family

Perhaps one of the juiciest subjects to dissect with people-ideal is circle of relatives. From being a mum who places her children first to being 'tremendous' to maintain the peace – there is lots of people-captivating that is occurring interior households. As kids, we're rewarded for our 'right' behaviour, and punished for being 'bad'. Perhaps you've been emotionally blackmailed or threatened via a member of the family to fulfill their needs and expectations, or invited people you've in no way met for your wedding ceremony at the request of your partner and children. Isn't it charming that, in a space in which we 'should' automatically belong, lots of our belonging and reputation is conditional? No wonder humans-fascinating has come to be synonymous with circle of relatives life!

Reflection Point: Take a 2nd to keep in mind your circle of relatives. Where do you human beings please, and who do you people please with? Do you recognise why?

Family dynamics may be the maximum complex (and poisonous) of all relationships. Intergenerational trauma keeps down the lineage, frequently rooted in mother (and father) wounds which can be repeated until the cycle is broken.

The Mother Wound

The Mother Wound is the ache of being a lady surpassed down thru generations of girls in patriarchal cultures. And it consists of the dysfunctional coping mechanisms which may be used to manner that ache.'~ Bethany Webster

Many women I comprehend (clients and friends) who magnificence themselves as people-pleasers have (or have had) a complicated courting with their mother. I'm no exception. My courting with my mum has comprised a myriad of fractured emotions. As properly as experiencing my private pain from kids, I can now appearance lower back at my mother's enjoy and see the techniques that she struggled too. For instance, I can now see that she positioned her very non-public dreams final plenty of the time. I can in spite of the truth that pay interest - and extra importantly, experience - the effect of her phrases: 'I in no way do what I want, I typically positioned you children first.' Seeing her citing 3 kids with this ringing in my ears brought about quite a few guilt. Without a doubt, the sensation of preventing your mother from having the existence she genuinely desired is heavy. When we've had been given a people-beautiful girl who we version our international on in our children, turning into a people-pleaser ourselves may be inevitable. Additionally, when you have a discern who tasks their dissatisfaction and unhappiness, you discover ways to experience accountable for their feelings. You devise techniques to make their lifestyles tons less complex and happier, consequently getting into a co-established people-charming relationship dynamic. Once I realised the likely poisonous effect this dynamic also can want to have on my own little one, I emerge as decided to break the cycle. The Mother Wound desires to be healed. If I can keep away from passing that burden without delay to my youngsters, I will. I recognize you do no longer need absolutely everyone on your existence to revel in that burden both.

Patty says: 'I haven't any doubt that the concept of human beings-appealing commenced as a totally young infant. I changed into the fourth of five siblings and my parents had been very strict. I grew up in New York in a completely Irish, Catholic neighbourhood and attended Catholic school. I observed to live thru manner of regulations and, as long as you followed the guidelines, you'll be rewarded. My mother and father were not very loving parents. They had been usually preventing.

We did no longer have a very heat, loving environment to grow up in. It changed right right into a kind of each-guy-for-himself environment. So, as a survival mechanism, I observed out a way to collect love via way of doing topics that made humans happy, and in pass again determined a few self-worth, love and interest. The beginning of human beings attractive. This concept of people-captivating have turn out to be past family; it additionally included instructors, friends, neighbours and plenty of others.'

This is a exquisite region to check the significance of the primary caregiver's characteristic on a infant and whether or not or no longer that affects the need to please as you get older. Bowlby's Theory of Attachment (developed and subtle thru the 20 th century) cites three attachment behaviours: regular, traumatic-resistant and avoidant. Mary Ainsworth superior these theories following research with more youthful toddlers and their number one caregivers to report the reaction of the youngsters at the same time as their number one caregiver a) left the studies space and b) lower again. If the toddler have been given visibly disenchanted upon their caregiver leaving however become with out troubles comforted on their go back, this end up classed as solid attachment. If the little one emerge as distressed even as their caregiver left and have become difficult to assuage on their skip again, and displaying conflicting behaviours, this modified into classed as nerve-racking-resistant. If the toddler have become now not overly distressed on their number one care giver leaving and actively prevented touch with them on their return, this have become classed as avoidant. (To explore this in addition, I propose the ebook Patterns of Attachment (Psychology Press & Routledge Classic Editions), thru Mary Ainsworth.)

From the Nineteen Eighties onwards, there has been big research into whether or not or now not or not the ones attachment behaviours as kids have an effect on our adult relationships. If we endure in mind how the mind works (as mentioned in financial catastrophe 1), a bit of research in 2018 on character attachment principle indicates they do: 'If we expect that person relationships are attachment relationships, it's miles viable that children who're strong as youngsters will enlarge as lots as be stable in their romantic relationships. Or, relatedly, that people who are strong as adults in their relationships with their dad and mom is probably more likely to forge sturdy relationships with new companions.'

The primary caregiver does no longer must be the mom but predominately it is. Attachment idea have become based totally at the vital that more youthful mammals aren't able to feed or protect themselves; they may be relying on their primary caregiver to satisfy the ones desires. If the number one caregiver is nearby and to be had (which, in people, also technique emotionally available and self-regulated), the child feels secure to play and find out feeling steady. When the number one caregiver isn't to be had to satisfy their wishes, the child enters a physiological state of survival; it doesn't experience secure.

People-appealing is some thing we test so that you can 'live on'. As Patty stated in advance, studying to get preserve of love thru doing matters that made human beings happy end up a survival mechanism. With a loss of consistent attachment, she devised a way to get hold of the self-worth, love and interest that she had to benefit an illusional enjoy of protection.

Children who experience regular are in a function to reveal all their feelings at the identical time as now not having to cover them; it's constant for them to carry out that. Anxious-resistant or avoidant youngsters have a tendency to repress their emotions or be crushed and all-fed on thru using them. As a humans-pleaser, you may recognize the latter in your self.

Rhona shared a number of her story with me, and it's one which can resonate with you. From early young people, Rhona modified into continuously in comparison to her cousin with the resource of her mum. Her cousin modified into, in Rhona's phrases, 'Perfect in each manner, behaviour, university, grades, seems — everything! I spent years wishing I have emerge as her and may be as wonderful as her in my mum's eyes.'

How unhappy that a more youthful woman spent years of her life wishing she was a person else. How many younger humans try this? How many younger people develop up wishing they had been a person else - a person extra smart, prettier, chattier, funnier, better behaved - so one can make their parents satisfied? By being in assessment to her cousin, Rhona misplaced who she changed into (albeit speedy) as a manner to delight her mum. Woah - what a difficult family dynamic! What end up Rhona's mum's motivation on this? Was she actually happier as speedy as Rhona moulded herself into a more perfect version?

Rhona's mum could have had to do a little vital digging into how she felt about herself before she may additionally moreover need to turn out to be glad with some thing. To be no longer capable of sincerely be given your daughter for who she is or, as a minimum, to understand how damaging evaluation is in your little one calls for a huge dollop of attention. When dad and mom are unaware and unconscious, that is the end result. Your infant has to do the paintings for themselves, for you, and for the generations before.

If Rhona had now not completed the recuperation artwork, her existence is probably very particular now. Instead of being aware of her human beings pleaser, she can be subconscious of her movements and to how she feels bodily, emotionally and spiritually. Without doing the artwork to permit bypass of the human beings pleaser, she can be preserving onto a whole lot of anxiety in her body. For example, whilst you keep directly to human beings-fascinating, your shoulders, decrease decrease lower back and hips can enjoy tight with tension. Emotionally, she might be like a jack-in-the-box, maintaining onto resentment, overwhelm, and in no way able to particular herself simply – till a few aspect would set her off and she or he need to leap out, complete of unprocessed anger. Spiritually, she would possibly disconnect and now not meet self-fulfilment (or self-actualisation as regular with Maslow's Hierarchy of Needs in bankruptcy 1) that is a part of our cause in this human experience.

Of route, the impact of humans best doesn't forestall with as. It ripples to the people around us, mainly our children. Without doing the recuperation work, the impact on Rhona's youngsters may want to were massive. They may have grown up choosing up her human beings attractive behavior, or casually time-commemorated (commonly via subconscious cues) that women have a responsibility to position their needs last.

This, again, reinforces elements:

1) How vital it is to your physical, emotional and non secular increase to permit go of people attractive. If you don't, dis-ease may additionally additionally furthermore occur on your frame. Your emotional health will go through, you'll war to connect with your intuition, and also you'll miss out on possibilities to unique your purpose.

Chapter 6: Father Relationship

When I did a few social research and asked, 'When come to be the concept of humans charming strengthened consciously or unconsciously indoors you?' 90% of ladies traced their humans fascinating decrease again to searching the love, approval, and validation that they did now not get from their father – that constant, kind, unconditional masculine presence changed into missing or skewed for plenty humans-pleasers.

As Shelley shares: 'From a totally younger age, my emotional dreams have been now not met. My father persevered to position me down and inform me I modified into thick and stupid. I turned into desperately looking to get my father to love me. My vanity became very low, and I assumed, at a younger age, that I was unlovable. I spent years seeking to please others and get them to love me.'

If your need to be preferred and customary of through way of a strong masculine have emerge as missing, you can find out your self (as an grownup) putting everyone else's desires earlier than your very personal. You might also moreover additionally are trying to find a 'father-parent' in a relationship and do the whole thing you could to pleasure and keep him. You can also enter a relationship with someone who has comparable inclinations on your father, despite the fact that they will be abusive. You can also moreover run your self ragged inside the regular desire that you will get the affection, approval and validation that grow to be lacking. The path and intensity that takes will depend on whether or now not or not that masculine presence grow to be missing, far flung, disapproving or abusive.

Without doing the paintings to unpack your humans-adorable tale and to apprehend your triggers, the cycle is prepared to copy all once more. And all all over again. And once more.

I changed into in that cycle of searching out someone to provide me the affection, approval and validation that I disregarded from my father. My father modified proper into a aggregate of abusive, remote and fantastically interested. The sexual abuse turned into covert. The emotional abuse grow to be excessive. For a long term, I bounced from semi-relationship to semi-relationship with guys who had been either one or each. I should attract guys who have been in some unspecified time in the future of me one minute and cold and remote the subsequent. On the other hand, I might likely pick men who've been emotionally unavailable and then spend time and strength deliberating a manner to get their hobby. My lowest element have become when I went again to someone who had date raped me. I did now not don't forget myself to be a sufferer; I concept those relationships have been what I modified into worth of. I have become moreover adept at hiding warning symptoms and symptoms and signs from others – properly knowledgeable from early life and simplest portray the picture to buddies that I favored them to look.

That cycle became set to replicate until I have become inclined to break it. I had to experience a whole lot of discomfort to do that. However, that pain modified into higher than the possibility.

More studies is growing now approximately the impact of pop-toddler relationships. Learning about Adverse Childhood Experiences (ACEs) placed masses in perspective approximately the effect my father had had on me (despite the fact that ACEs relate to all parental figures).

The data of ACEs started out out with ten questions based spherical critiques like abuse, domestic violence, loss of protection, and substance misuse in early life. More questions have eventually prolonged the profile. When I did the preliminary ten questions, my score have emerge as eight. My score have become quite revelatory, regardless of the reality that I modified into properly aware of the bad, dysfunctional environment I modified into raised in.

A 0.33 of all highbrow health situations in adults are right now associated with terrible formative years research. Having four or greater ACEs ought to have a big psychological effect on you as a toddler and, even as carried into maturity, can bring about excessive health troubles, substance misuses, and similarly. Without popularity and the proper remedy had to heal, the cycle also can keep.

As formative as our relationships with our parents or number one care givers are, it's miles possible to create the resilience, solid attachment and self-love that changed into eroded through an bad formative years. As referred to in monetary wreck 1, neuroplasticity technique that we can create new neural connections in our thoughts and, eventually, more tremendous consequences. We have already looked at the super recuperation electricity of meditation and mindfulness. Having skilled ACEs and no longer the use of a concept of those ideas on the time, my procedures to create resilience, constant attachment and self-love as an person have blanketed:

Therapy. This modified into vital for my emotional recuperation. It stays important for my well-being. It gives me with a steady area to speak, cry, and heal.

Yoga. My lifeline for my reconnection to my body thru re-analyzing a way to respire and a way to open my body again up. Still my favored way to return again to myself.

Various energy-recuperation modalities. These supported my important reconnection to Source.

I communicate in my paintings approximately your internal and outdoor guide systems. Both are similarly vital and manual your restoration and increase. Externals include treatment, counselling, and strength healers. It's so essential which you find the right character to art work with. Take some time and be aware of your instinct approximately who is going to help you. Get some consultations in advance than making a decision on a therapist, visit a drop-in beauty earlier than you pre-ebook a block of yoga instructions, and take a look at in with the critiques and credentials of the power healers you are trying to find to artwork with. And, probable more importantly, do make certain that your therapist is trauma-knowledgeable, or as a minimum has a remarkable jogging records of trauma. This may additionally sound apparent, however, you'd be surprised what number of people do now not have this understanding and recognition, and who therefore hazard re-traumatising their customers.

Chapter 7: Parenting

Throughout this e book we've touched upon parenting and the manner our humans attractive can impact our youngsters, and the subsequent forms of behaviour which can be repeated if we do not do the inner art work. We've looked at evolutionary technology and those stunning as a survival method, and we've taken into consideration the difference among humans lovely and co-operation, in addition to raising youngsters who're kind in preference to 'fantastic'. In this financial ruin, we are going to take the focus far from your children and take a look at parenting from a one-of-a-kind attitude: you and your function as a decide.

Let's be sincere – parenting isn't usually clean. Some parents discover a new determined self notion and enjoy of cause even as we have had been given children while others lose our self perception (and ourselves). Many humans input into parenthood sincerely unprepared for the fact which not regularly suits our pre-toddler romanticised notions of the manner it's miles going to be. There's nothing quite like birthing new existence into the world to force you to face your demons!

Nowadays, besides we pick out out an opportunity approach, healthcare professionals have hundreds more input and manipulate over our youngsters (and our frame) from the immediately we find out we're pregnant. This isn't a criticism, more a reflected image of the manner times (and remedy) have changed. Where as quickly as we'd have on the whole been guided by way of the use of our natural instincts and instinct, now we appearance to the outdoor and the plethora of frequently conflicting recommendation and records. We prevent trusting ourselves and instead placed our believe inside the palms of experts and relative strangers. From a human beings appropriate mindset, this can appear like making picks based on others' reviews in place of paying attention to our innate understanding, dreams and desires. It can appear like doubting your intuition whilst in no manner thinking others' recommendation.

Later on, human beings pleasing can appear like getting your toddler Christened due to the reality a relative expects you to (no matter the reality which you aren't a part of the Christian faith); or not placing limitations at the same time as your infant is born, as an alternative resentfully allowing genuinely everybody to go to whilst what you really need is bonding time collectively in conjunction with your little one.

It's easy to get the message that the whole thing we're doing as a determine is inaccurate. This is difficult for the humans pleaser who wishes ordinary validation that we're doing subjects proper. Instead, we frequently find out ourselves crippled with self-doubt even as looking for to create the façade that we've got got everything together!

People charming as a decide takes many office work:

Not advocating in your little one while confronted via circle of relatives contributors, friends, specific dad and mom and teachers about their behaviour

Trying to micro-manipulate and manipulate your little one's behaviour so you can control one-of-a-kind humans's belief of them and, perhaps greater pertinent, different humans's perception of you and your parenting ability (whats up, innerCONTROLfreak!)

Saying sure to playdates even as you need to mention no, or not seeking to depart a party early due to the reality you don't need to seem impolite (despite the truth that your exceedingly-touchy introverted little one is decided for some quiet time!)

Hiding who you sincerely are with extraordinary dad and mom (and possibly ingesting to more to numb social anxiety at social sports!)

Sacrificing your integrity and values certainly so you can 'healthy in' with remarkable dad and mom

Spending Christmas and particular 'special' events with prolonged own family while you actually need to spend it by myself along with your partner and children

Performative parenting, i.E. Converting your parenting fashion because of the truth people are searching

Not speakme up toward pals/own family who're making complex remarks in the front of your children, e.G. About their look/weight, racist or homophobic feedback and so on

Advocating and being the voice for your infant is perhaps one of the maximum difficult things to do as a humans pleaser. On the only hand, as deeply sensitive, compassionate beings, you recognize that your infant is worth and deserving of understand, and to be acquainted and nurtured for who they're, warts and all. On the alternative hand, your need to be desired and well-known way that occasionally it's less difficult to conform with the recognition quo without assignment. However, children want to apprehend that at the least one individual in their life has their once more, no matter what. This doesn't advise that they aren't held answerable for their movements. But it does suggest that they may be approached with empathy and compassion, and are given permission to make mistakes. Children are, in the long run, human – just like us! Also, with the useful resource of advocating for our kids (and with the aid of our children bearing witness to this), they discover ways to suggest for themselves. The greater they could suggest for themselves, the much less they'll look to others for approval.

Reflection Point: Looking on the listing above, are you able to emerge as aware of in which you have had been given humans thrilled as a decide? Why do you need to transport faraway from this now?

Chapter 8: Friendships

As we mature, thru childhood and into our early twenties, our friendships end up as vital as our circle of relatives relationships as we are able to decide and pick who we spend time with. Friendships - at their fantastic - can nurture and uplift you, supplying you with emotional manual as well as allowing you to reciprocate that emotional help. However, friendships can on occasion revel in one-sided or based mostly on unfair expectancies, mainly in case your people pleaser can be very energetic in your relationship!

Rachel shared: 'I may constantly exit of my way to do subjects for human beings but usually felt like I in no manner were given the identical lower back from pals. I had a deep feeling of anger in me however I in no manner knew why or wherein it came from. I may always snap or make passive aggressive comments, and then feel truely stupid and stew on them for a while after.'

Relatable, proper? How frequently do you go out of your manner due to the fact you are trying to satisfaction someone? It might possibly seem like you're being 'exquisite' however definitely it's now not coming from a sincere place. This is at the same time as we want to be considerably honest with ourselves about our purpose and intention. For example; you provide to permit your buddy stay for a few days while her residence is being repainted. If your motive is, 'My mate goes to be so grateful and like me hundreds extra for this,' instead of, 'I need to help, and it is probably exceptional to spend a chunk of greater time collectively,' then you definitely are attaching to an very last consequences counting on something you may't manipulate. It is you seeking to govern that person. The 2nd purpose is coming out of your preference to assist. So, better to now not be 'amazing' and as a substitute be honest. If you provide a few element, allow it come out of your reality.

Of course, if you experience you've got were given provided some element with a honest, right motivation and also you do no longer sense favored, there might be a boundary to be checked out. An honest conversation explaining the way you revel in, or making a decision to do some thing one-of-a-type within the destiny, will enhance your choice now not to humans please. This isn't always approximately being a doormat or about feeling unappreciated. It is a desire you're making to reveal up the manner that feels right to you in every friendship.

Going above and past, at times, may be a stunning issue, but take a look at in if you revel in a enjoy of responsibility, or that it's being demanded of you. If you're feeling obligated or in call for, it's miles coming from a place of expectation.

There are friendships wherein you can have completed that role for see you later that an expectation has been made on you to be a powerful way. Changing this dynamic might be disruptive – a few human beings gained't apprehend the 'new' you. Keeping it, regardless of the fact that, is destructive. I can promise you that, as you hold running thru the 7-Step Exploration, you won't need to stay on your people captivating function to hold the popularity quo.

In monetary catastrophe 1 we in short touched at the people-appealing dynamics – victim, martyr (rescuer) and, for the dynamic to paintings, the offender (oppressor). This is known as the drama triangle. The drama triangle is a model of social interplay that maps negative interactions happening amongst people, specially in struggle. We all assume each 'function' at numerous tiers in our lives.

In a few friendships, specifically the ones wherein we have got set ourselves up due to the reality the victim or martyr from the beginning, our 'pal' assumes the characteristic of the culprit. This doesn't endorse that we revel in abuse from them, but, they keep the power and manage inside the friendship. Their goals and desires dominate your very non-public which, quite frankly, performs right away into the fingers of your human beings pleaser! It becomes pretty the reciprocal courting – your buddy allows your want to thrill at the same time as you validate their oppressive energy. In those friendships, you could 'cut lower back' or blur into the historic past even as your pal takes centre diploma. When you're every single and dating, you take a backseat, assuming that everyone will like your friend anyway. You're reluctant to voice your opinion, as an opportunity agreeing with theirs, or discover which you don't surely have a voice.

As you grow in self assurance, find your voice, and start to rate yourself more, the ones are the very relationships that begin to fall away. The dynamic changes; you're not the martyr or the sufferer (and the 'perpetrator' needs each to stay on). So, you become surplus to requirements. The cease of a friendship is difficult, despite the fact that the relationship turn out to be volatile. With a shared information, and an entire identification built round it, the loss of a friend can convey up emotions of grief, anger, rejection and betrayal. No recollect the connection or conditions, permit yourself to sense all of the feelings.

It is now your desire to pick out not to human beings please. As you'll see in the intimate relationships economic spoil, if someone wishes you to be satisfied, they may recognize the changes you are making. If now not, it wasn't a supportive, reciprocal courting.

Chapter 9: Intimate Relationships

While we regularly consider intercourse while we consider intimacy, what we truly propose is closeness (we'll communicate sex within the next financial disaster!). Being intimate with someone manner being prone, permitting them into your coronary coronary heart and sharing all of you, even the darkish and messy elements. Of direction, that is like kryptonite for your human beings pleaser (and ego), as it approach stepping out from in the lower back of the mask.

In my intimate dating, that is wherein my human beings pleaser loves to maintain out the maximum. Through massive (and fairly painful) studies, I determined that there are 3 layers to the people pleaser. For me, the expertise sunk in after I did the 7-Step Exploration – I realised that I had picked up people applicable as a defence mechanism/coping approach for being in a wholesome and supportive dating. Rather than permitting my truth to come out, humans fascinating enabled me to stay 'stable' inside the dating thru hiding the components of me that I notion is probably rejected.

The three layers are unique to intimate relationships, notwithstanding the reality that you could realise them in exceptional relationships as properly. You will see how human beings beautiful indicates up thru the ones layers, affecting conversation, your ranges of happiness, your functionality to experience satisfaction, and your standard wellbeing. I am focusing this section at the manner you enjoy. I will add, however, that a fantastic component effect is a better enjoy within the relationship for your partner. However, if the relationship isn't proper or stable for you, then please don't stay and assume you sincerely want to do greater paintings. I surely need that in case you aren't within the right courting this bankruptcy will help you understand that it's time to go away.

As you read approximately each layer, get clean on wherein you take a seat internal every, and get prepared to use the antidote – Put Yourself First.

1) The first layer is: YOU ARE MORE IMPORTANT THAN I AM

This layer is placing the other man or woman's goals above your private. This is the complex region to begin. When you grow to be privy to your humans pleaser, you'll be aware the locations wherein your people pleaser indicates up. When you emerge as privy to your mind, moves and ideals in your intimate relationship (or a potential one), you may see the way you continuously located that person's dreams earlier than your very non-public.

In this deposit, you do now not recognize the manner to articulate what you want. You will most probable be having communique issues to your intimate courting and you'll be pushing all of the ones feelings down.

This is your reminder: Your self-worth can in no way be confirmed through in reality all and sundry else. Take lower back your electricity, and prevent searching forward to someone else to make you experience better approximately a few issue. The first step to taking decrease again your strength in your intimate courting is to peel lower back this number one layer and apply the antidote – Put Yourself First.

Your partner (most possibly) does now not need you to second-wager what they want, and in reality goals you in truth to be you. If they do not need that, they may be not the proper individual for you. This is going for EVERY dating. If the person you're people appealing sulks, stops talking to you, and wishes that you skip lower decrease back to the 'vintage' you at the same time as you start using the people fascinating antidote, then they do now not have your terrific pastimes. It is up to you to decide if your energy is splendid used on that courting (or now not).

2) The 2nd layer is: I CAN ONLY BE HAPPY WITH YOU

Good antique co-dependency. This is in which you understand you're looking forward to all your fulfilment to pop out of your companion. You have lost sight of what it's want to have fun out of doors of your dating, and there may be immoderate jealousy on the concept of your partner doing something without you.

You will discover yourself announcing 'I'm satisfactory' on a normal foundation, which, as , is seldom the case. You understand if you utter the words 'I'm first rate' then it proper away manner that you're now not. At all. Using this word excellent serves to make you experience worse – you grow to be a seething pool of unexpressed emotion, driven way down and plastered over with recollections of methods you want to make the other man or woman satisfied to be everyday. In this accretion, despite the fact that the feelings will spring up, you are not capable of tool them.

Again, you need to apply the antidote proper right here – Put Yourself First. You want to be willing to discover how you will be happy to your own. Yes, it's feasible, I PROMISE you! This have to appear to be a time body on your very personal, using your internal assist systems to do what you need to. You most clearly need to approach your feelings and your desires.

three) The 1/3 layer is: WHAT DO I ACTUALLY WANT FROM YOU + ME

The zero.33 layer is all approximately intercourse and intimacy.

Opening myself as loads as intimacy became one of the maximum inclined things I surely have ever completed. I prevented intimacy and as a substitute used strategies to numb myself from being gift with myself. These procedures meant I should in no way REALLY listen to what I desired and desired within the 2nd.

In this deposit, the intimacy starts offevolved offevolved with you. How are you inclined to get to understand you?

I didn't even apprehend how a whole lot of my strength have become ate up with micro-managing everyone else's happiness till I began to unpick it, no longer as a martyr or sufferer, however as someone who merits the maximum in love and compassion. And positive, certainly, love and compassion begins offevolved with the way you pay interest and communicate to YOU. Once you're in an notable courting with your self, the humans charming has to prevent – you won't tolerate it for yourself anymore.

I think a number of the most important lessons I actually have found out and achievements I really have made have been in my intimate dating. Truthfully, it's miles messy and painful going via the layers ... and then to be willing to move even deeper. The work in no way stops.

Being your health warrior is vital to helping yourself in your adventure to ditching your people pleaser. You should recognize what you want and whilst you need it to preserve your 'bucket' complete. Depletion and crush will see you slipping back into the vintage styles of human beings charming. Being your nicely-being warrior is bespoke for your frame, breath and Soul. This manner you want to get clear on what your Essential Me Time Maintenance (EMTM) seems like each day. EMTM includes yourself-care, on and rancid the mat exercising, plus your inner and out of doors assist structures. It moreover way self-speak and boundaries. You need your Essential Me Time

Maintenance that will help you within the route of the month, and to work collectively along with your personal cycle and/or the moon cycle – as your power changes and shifts, you want to paintings with that electricity, now not in opposition to it. Most importantly, on the identical time as it is adorable to understand yourself and what you want, none of that subjects if you aren't really doing it! Tap into your antidote - Put Yourself First - and installation your EMTM to do the things that make you feel appropriate.

Chapter 10: Love, Sex And Sexuality

If we didn't get hold of the love and connection that we wished growing up, or had been raised with an traumatic or avoidant attachment, it's no longer unusual to are looking for them through dangerous technique. Sex is some factor that can outcomes be 'traded' for romance, however fleeting the on the spot. While sex in itself isn't horrible – suitable day, it could be the most magical and delightful enjoy – at the same time as the intention inside the back of it comes from a place of lack of self warranty and want for validation, we can be left feeling empty and plenty plenty much less lovable, often desiring more intercourse to revel in extra lovely, for that reason stepping into a destructive cycle. We may additionally additionally discover ourselves agreeing to sex acts that make us experience uncomfortable, or relationships that enjoy risky, clearly to be favored (or cherished) greater. Overtime, we are capable of growth a warped enjoy of sex that can impact our intimate relationships afterward.

Love + Sex

Wrapped up in expectation and validation are love and intercourse. 10 years in the beyond, I need to have run away at the concept of sharing my feelings within the route of intercourse with you. I did now not apprehend a manner to do intercourse. Physical and emotional pain left me feeling trapped. I needed to numb myself to have sex, and I never had an orgasm. I changed into in preferred worry and believed that I have turn out to be intrinsically damaged. Love and sex to people pleasers is something we crave however further fear. I suppose it's honest to anticipate that anybody have a story round love and intercourse.

I became 16. I had actually spent the night time with my then boyfriend in a consensual sexual scenario (I will spare you the teenage records). I felt utter disgrace. Disgust. Hatred. I near down even in addition. The story commenced out to head deeper. 'I am damaged. I am incorrect.' The first time I had intercourse I cried and cried. The physical ache turn out to be excruciating, and the wave of emotional pain became uncontrollable. I didn't understand the way to articulate what became taking vicinity. It wasn't a one-off. So, alcohol have turn out to be an important crutch to be 'regular' within the path of sex aka to Not Be Sensitive. I wasn't able to articulate to others or myself the abuse I had expert as a infant. What determined in the coming years modified into date rape and a chain of toxic relationships. I even went again to the accomplice who had date raped me. That modified into how institutionalised my human beings appealing became.

The change passed off after I started to train as a yoga teacher. I resisted meditation for so long as I ought to, as I knew I did no longer want to get quiet with myself. Then, one night time, I realised I couldn't face up to it any greater. I became uninterested in constantly ignoring myself and drowning out the entirety. I pondered. And the words got here: 'You had been abused by way of way of manner of your father whilst you have been seven.' I broke down. For more than one days, I end up in a weird limbo of remedy and despair. To apprehend what I typically knew and so that you can face it modified into each a warfare of phrases and surrender. Counselling and treatment have supported me to launch the trauma across the abuse, and to get to some extent in which I can rebuild my relationship round love and intercourse.

My courting with my father must in no way be rebuilt. He rejected me time and time another time, and the priority around that stayed even as he left. For human beings pleasers to release the antique tales round love and intercourse takes try. To launch the ache takes energy. Many parents have expert trauma. It won't have been sexual trauma but, as a touchy character, you could have absorbed trauma. By shutting down your sensitivity, that trauma could had been held on your body.

I am not a trauma therapist. I am not a therapist or counsellor. If any clients disclose to me that they have got experienced abuse or trauma, I suggest them to paintings with a educated expert. They have the crucial strategies and education. How I assist people, however, is via harnessing the energy in their sensitivity - compassion, braveness and connection - in art work, purpose, relationships, and the usage of their voice, and thru connecting with their body, thoughts and soul. Many recuperation modalities awareness at the thoughts, which has its location, of direction. However, recuperation from trauma calls for a somatic method. If you don't work with a counsellor or trauma professional, then I could advocate the use of your breath - some component each person have get right of entry to to - in addition to frame work as a part of your exercise. This is what I do, even nowadays. My workout is my helpline, my anchor – it had been given me via and gets me through a lot.

When you connect with your breath - your breath that has been held for a totally long time; the breath you suppress so you can do all the topics for honestly everyone else - you launch tension, stress, anxiety and fear. You re-learn how to be present. As a people pleaser, it's essential which you supply yourself decrease once more Into the right here and now. Using your breath, you could allow cross of the maintain the beyond has on you, even only for a second, and release the priority of the future. Your breath creates location on your body and thoughts, allowing you to get right of entry to that deep unwavering love for your self.

Love Languages

If you're acquainted with the art work of Gary Chapman, you will apprehend that he has diagnosed five languages that we speak (particularly non-verbally) that permit us to revel in loved. Understanding our dominant love language and that of our accomplice can decorate our communique and courting. The 5 love languages are summarised beneath. If you would love to discover those in greater intensity, I can recommend Gary's e-book, The five Love Languages.

Words of Affirmation

This love language expresses love thru powerful phrases and includes verbal compliments and the remarkable of reward. Negative phrases and complaint will damage a person with this dominant love language.

Quality Time

This love language is prepared undivided interest and being gift to someone without distractions. Postponing time with or not being present to a person whose love language is incredible time may be dangerous.

Receiving Gifts

A enormous or thoughtful present makes a person with this dominant love language sense desired. They additionally have a tendency to present others as an expression in their love. Forgetting birthdays or now not placing concept into a gift, which can be as easy as surprising them with their favored bar of chocolate, can go away someone with this dominant love language feeling unappreciated.

Acts of Service

This love language expresses itself via way of the use of doing topics with superb motive and together in conjunction with your companion's happiness in mind. This doesn't consist of movements out of responsibility or with a terrible tone. Someone with this dominant love language would require their partner to be receptive in their company, and now not too stubborn or independent to collect it.

Physical Touch

People with this love language feel associated and strong in a relationship thru keeping palms, hugging and kissing and so forth. A loss of bodily touch can leave them touch-starved and feeling rejected.

As human beings pleasers, we are more likely to preserve types of co-dependency inside our relationships, making ourselves answerable for the desires and emotions of others. In phrases of the love languages, relationships are reinforced whilst each partners reciprocate the love language of the possibility. If we make the effort to spend fantastic time with our associate, for example, but they don't honour our language of receiving items, communication breaks down, our wishes are omitted, and we can become inexperienced with envy.

Of route, absolutely every body want to take duty for our very non-public wishes, and for voicing whilst our wishes are being neglected via our associate – we can not assume anybody to take a look at our mind! There is, but, a totally pleasant line between co-dependency and interdependence, the latter meaning that we non-public our emotions, take duty for assembly our very very own desires (with out putting the onus on everybody else to meet them) AND lean on our companion for emotional manual. Relationships are (purported to be) an equal partnership that calls for deliver, take and attention on every factors. Knowing the language in that you most feel loved, and attempting your associate to understand and honour it, doesn't make you insecure or needy. It in reality approach that it's the expression that most resonates and allows you to talk (and get hold of) love more effectively and authentically.

Michelle says: 'As a reformed human beings pleaser, my love language is affirmations. Growing up I changed into praised for my educational achievement and creative competencies. In reality, it modified into the most effective time that I heard a few issue super stated approximately me without a few horrible once more-passed undertone (which, I'm positive, we are capable of all resonate with as sensitives). So, I internalised this praise as love. My partner, inside the meantime, needs bodily touch to experience cherished – no longer smooth once I find contact sensory-overload a number of the time. At one factor, he and I had a breakdown in conversation. I realised that neither humans have become speaking the other's love language. While we're very interdependent and recognize that we're not accountable for each awesome, we now consciously spend a hint time each day to speak the opportunity's love language. He offers me phrases of encouragement, specially as quickly as I'm feeling tired or down, and I display bodily affection (albeit as a super deal as I can bodily tolerate).'

My love language is likewise terms of confirmation. I enjoy listening to things like I even have completed an tremendous hobby, or I actually have made someone sense satisfied. For humans pleasers, those form of terms of affirmation are the proverbial cherry on the cake! We truely need to get better at listening to ourselves say the ones phrases to our self.

A General Note on Rejection

Rejection can experience painful, a lot virtually so we do whatever we are able to to keep away from it (that is the correct bait for your humans pleaser). Nobody desires to experience rejected; we don't want similarly evidence of the way 'now not enough' we are. However, avoiding the pain through manner of looking for to outsmart rejection at every turn is arduous and wastes your immeasurable talents and energy.

One survival approach that human beings pleasers undertake is to make themselves majorly amenable. Another is to come to be crucial. Outrunning rejection turns into a skills, but even as you do experience rejection as a people pleaser, it floors you. I actually have turn out to be devastated at the same time as a person I had dated some times ghosted me. 'What must I really have performed in each different way?' 'What have become wrong with me?' Repeatedly, I replayed numerous situations and countless motives for the rejection in my thoughts. All of the blame landed on me. Probably, he became a bit of a douche and didn't want the problem of texting to mention he wasn't involved. However, I made all of it about me. I'd accomplished some element wrong. I wasn't appropriate sufficient. The rejection lessen deep; it felt so non-public.

Fast earlier to last one year and I determined that pretty a few ladies who've been early participants of a set I ran had unfriended me on Facebook. This time, I didn't take the rejection for my part. I knew that my being extra vocal about social troubles together with racism wasn't landing with a few people; it wasn't the message they have been prepared (or attempting) to pay interest. And that's ok. I remained curious but wasn't emotionally linked to their rejection of me; I knew it modified into as loads a part of their adventure as it emerge as mine. I not preferred their validation – a massive win for any people pleaser! The difference came from liberating my want to pleasure on a every day foundation. Little via little, the validation I now have for myself - being my very non-public wonderful friend and assisting me - manner my outlook has shifted. Now, I'm no longer going to faux that if I have become majorly rejected now that it wouldn't damage. I'm human. I'm sensitive. And, along with you, I experience the whole lot. The difference now might be that I harness my sensitivity and emotional popularity as a present in preference to allowing myself to enjoy pressured by the usage of them.

Chapter 11: Women Misogynists

The New Wave of feminism submit #metoo has heralded a ultra-modern area or (permit us to be honest) a promise of a brand new place for women to take residency. However, patriarchy, humans-fascinating, structural racism, and internalised misogyny are although so prolific because of unconscious bias that it's far difficult to non-public the ones areas completely.

I acquired't flow into structural racism. I'm no longer an professional on intersectional feminism and structural racism, and for the have a check of this, I might probably urge you to are trying to find out BIPOC teachers (see the assets section behind this ebook for the educators I actually have determined from). Racism is deeply entrenched, and white people have a obligation to educate ourselves and observe our non-public biases. I do, but, want to take a second to speak approximately girls who display misogynistic tendencies, mind and behaviours. These perpetuate humans-stunning. When ladies do not enjoy supported with the aid of the utilization of various girls - via negative reports or lack of women round them - the beliefs they have got grown up with are internalised into misogyny alongside the misogynistic notions from records and famous culture. A lot of misogyny is internalised as disgrace which we then assignment onto different ladies (and our daughters), persevering with the misogynistic cycle.

We all have internalised misogyny within us, even though we think we do now not. Just take a second to pause and replicate on your mind-set in the direction of going for walks mums or live-at-domestic mums, as an instance. Perhaps you choose girls who pick no longer to have youngsters and/or girls who've 'extra than their sincere percent'. Do you claim to be a feminist however preserve prejudice towards trans women?

How do you view promiscuous women as opposed to promiscuous guys? Maybe you have had been given some of terrible concept around scantily clad girls, or perhaps girls carrying hijabs and covering their body from head-to-toe.

How do you enjoy approximately girls and their use of expletive language? I can assure that you have pretty a few terrible belief and opinion round ladies in comparison with guys, in particular in phrases of mothering, appearance and sexuality, and this is in advance than we add intersections which includes elegance, gender identification and race. You may not had been aware about your biases until I posed the questions simply now. Viewing ladies as some detail apart from identical to guys is a symptom of internalised misogyny.

Internalised misogyny furthermore plays out inside the diploma of our well actually really worth and the manner we show up and unique our self in the international. As a human beings-pleaser, on a few degree, you do now not endure in thoughts you, as a girl, are worthy of X genuinely because of the reality you are a lady. This isn't always any other hold on with beat yourself up with however an opportunity to reflect. Like any prejudice or bias, most of this lies in our subconscious mind. When I expect once more to times that I've people pleased, I believed (consciously) that I wasn't really worth of X, and (unconsciously) that I grow to be now not well worth of X due to the fact I modified into a girl.

Note: this isn't approximately being anti-man or announcing that 'all guys are arseholes'. When we endure in thoughts the patriarchy, as an instance, we're speakme approximately a device that favours and offers societal privileges to guys because of their gender. When we're talking approximately misogyny, we're speaking approximately an imbalance of power. Due to ancient and societal attitudes and ideals about ladies (how they 'ought to' be and the way they 'need to' behave), and thinking about the drama triangle as discussed in chapter 8, guys expect the dynamic of the 'wrongdoer' at the identical time as ladies grow to be the 'sufferer'. As girls, we've got were given internalised this dynamic and the related beliefs which means that we, too, view girls as 'a whole lot less than' (in the major unconsciously), projecting our non-public insecurities onto one of a kind girls on the same time as being blind to the dynamics at play.

Section 3: People Pleasing ... In Work

In this section, we're going to examine how the workplace way of life may be a fertile floor for people captivating. From my research into this problem depend it have emerge as obvious right away that, in case you end up privy to as a women, you're more likely to human beings please at paintings. Of route, there are plenty of ladies who do not people please. Likewise, men aren't immune from human beings appealing at paintings. However, at the danger of generalising, it seems to be greater of a women's hassle.

We are going to have a check what it approach to be fine in place of assertive for your art work area, and what happens at the same time as you're most important a team as a human beings pleaser. It appears that a number of the discrepancies among ladies and men at art work can be right proper right down to humans adorable expectations. Get geared up to mission how you are being at artwork, and task the work region tradition that rewards humans charming.

Chapter 12: The Post-Metoo Workplace

#Metoo, the decision for the gender pay hollow to be reduce, multiplied recognition of corporations' hiring practices, and place of work way of life name-outs have introduced an extended accountability to what's happening in our artwork environments. This expanded responsibility and hobby technique the discrepancies among ladies and men in the workplace have turn out to be glaringly obvious. So, why is there an expectation of you to pride people at paintings?

Sarah says: 'At paintings, I push myself and take on more obligations because of the reality there can be an expectation I will say sure. Years of feeling the pressure to be that man or woman who goes out of their manner to help can be emotionally laborious. Other people will argue about powerful topics on the identical time as I will certainly get on with them, whether or now not I agree or not – I don't want to purpose a fuss.'

Ah, the 'I don't want to purpose a fuss' scenario. We knew it changed into coming, right? In reality, few humans want to reason a fuss at paintings. But why does saying no or not being the handiest who volunteers for the whole lot should mean you're inflicting a fuss? Is this proper all the way down to feeling we've to expose ourselves so one may be time-honored at artwork? I need you to take a second to don't forget the unseen labour you do at artwork. Consider the electricity and strive you install to stumble upon as 'pleasant' and amenable. Do you spend time correcting the tone and language in your emails so you don't come upon as too 'bossy' or assertive? How approximately the conversations you rehearse for your head to soothe the person who motives you pressure at work? Perhaps you may see some of you in what Sarah has shared above – feeling emotionally exhausted and seeking to get through your day without 'inflicting a fuss'.

I'm now not announcing you need to walk into artwork the following day, inform everybody to fuck off, and sit down consuming crisps while browsing the net all day – that could be a effective manner to get fired! There is, of course, place of work etiquette. You have your precise obligations and recognize your contractual responsibilities and code of behavior. Besides, you in all likelihood experience interacting together along with your colleagues (some of them anyway), and need to preserve your interest! What I am suggesting is that you look at how a whole lot energy and try you're expending to humans please. There are different greater constructive strategies to invest your abilities, electricity and focus into your personal and professional improvement, and leisure.

A short word on authenticity and 'being actual'. What I'm approximately to percent can be implemented to any of the topics we've blanketed on this ebook so far but it feels pertinent to proportion it in this chapter. Authenticity is a phrase that receives banded spherical loads, especially on the same time as we're speaking approximately personal and expert improvement. 'Just be your self.' 'Just do you.' 'Be greater you.' Sound acquainted?

Before I skip on, I want to famend that for a few people, displaying up entire-heartedly as their actual self isn't steady. Some cultures are although unaccepting of homosexuality, for instance, on the identical time as a female may additionally adopt greater 'masculine' tendencies to revel in greater steady in a closely male-ruled environment. In the ones situations it's understandable why a few human beings have to disguise additives of themselves and might more consciously select to be amenable to others.

Being authentic is not pretty lots expressing who you're with out the want to cover within the again of a masks, or growing a greater socially right alter-ego. It's honestly not approximately being impolite and brash and telling anyone what you honestly think about them underneath the guise of being 'real'. But it is about regarding extra authentically to others within the way that we be part of and speak.

In the administrative center, there is usually a manner of life of pushing via, running more tough and longer, and wearing 'busy' as a badge of honour – quality ammo for human beings lovely! There is continually a boss, organization member, or worrying patron to be placated. Repeatedly working above and past on responsibilities, continuously appeasing tough group people, or accommodating honestly not possible requests because of the truth they're an vital patron – this manner of existence thrives on compete and test.

Does your achievement depend upon lovely others? Sadly, no. When we human beings please inside the place of job, we may also moreover additionally experience that that is giving us an advantage but pretty the opportunity is actual. The minute we turn out to be amenable is the minute we positioned a barrier up between our projected photograph and our true nature, which influences the way we relate to others. The people who normally tend to 'be triumphant' in the administrative center aren't usually the ones based totally on gain, but are often the ones who've created greater real connections with their colleagues and superiors.

There wants to be some quite seismic mindset adjustments to permit for humans cute to stop at artwork. You can make a contribution to alternate through your movements and ideals, and enhance how an awful lot you understand your self at paintings in preference to attempting to find validation from others.

Marike says: 'From my private experience as a girl in era, the times as quickly as I am being assertive or taking over a control function, people (almost generally guys) in my professional and private circles have commented on how I'm now not being first-rate enough, now not female, no longer ladylike, now not 'my candy self' and plenty of others. '

Michelle presents: 'I've had instances even as my hard work and similarly hours have lengthy past omitted, and no longer being vocal approximately how busy I am has impacted my rating within the bonus pool. I've waited for someone else to head away the administrative center first (even though it supposed missing my educate and being overdue home), and felt accountable for taking a time without work to look after my sick toddler. But, maximum drastically, are the times when I've stood up for what's proper. When I've spoken fact to strength. I've been labelled a problem maker often; it appears maximum of my jobs have desired the remarkable, quiet and amenable model of me.'

This is what you're going to rise up closer to – different human beings attempting you to be superb at paintings as it advantages them and upholds their reputation quo. It makes their life easier. Having compliant, easy going sure human beings in your organization, or as your employees, manner plenty plenty less problem. Are you organized to shake the guidelines through no longer being wonderful?

Remember: being amazing isn't similar to being type, and the autonym of exceptional isn't 'bitch' (despite the fact that, allow's face it, if you're not amenable as a female then you may be labelled such. Thank you, misogyny!).

Let's say Marike has discovered a state-of-the-art piece of research which contradicts the artwork of a member of her group. They have a conversation and the alternative character, allow's name them Jo, is hoping that Marike acquired't deliver it up at their next agency discussion. Jo, who's dismissive of the studies, reminds Marike how lots artwork might be created by way of the use of manner of introducing it. Marike has options:

a)   To be quality and now not deliver up this piece of studies. She is high-quality privy to Jo's mindset and might see how this can purpose warfare between them at paintings. She furthermore doesn't need to 'purpose a fuss'.

b)   To stick to what's right for her and to introduce this new piece of research.

If you were in the equal seize 22 situation, which preference should you select out?

The place of business is full of excellent Marikes and Michelles and, allow's face it, we adore them – they make lifestyles clean. But here's some contemporary records for in which we are at with women within the workplace within the UK. As of April 2019, there are not any sectors in the UK wherein ladies are paid the same as men, although they're doing exactly the equal pastime. None. Baffling that that is the twenty first century and that is the running landscape. (Source, Financial Times.)

I need to thing out that for black girls and girls of color this hole is even large. In the UK, ladies from minoritised groups don't even comprehend how large a pay gap they may be experiencing as corporations handiest damage it down via male and female. The Fawcett Society are currently mastering the problems surrounding black ladies and girls of colour inside the place of job. Alongside the pay hole, there are more than one different issues that black girls and girls of color face; such a whole lot of more issues that might make a contribution to the need to people please.

I'm not announcing that ditching your humans applicable will change those troubles. Deep reform and seismic mind-set adjustments are desired. Some subjects are changing, of direction. We have advanced beyond most effective being hired as secretaries inside the administrative center, or being predicted to renounce as soon as married, as modified into although the case for lots corporations within the 70s. There stays an prolonged way to transport, but. It stands to cause that in case you are a white female studying this and also you do the paintings on humans fascinating inside the place of job, you can moreover be doing the art work to guide women of shade to your place of work too. What aid are you able to provide? How are you capable of be an remarkable pal? Please check out the belongings segment at the back of this e-book for my recommendations on BIPOC educators who can help you with this.

What I am suggesting even though is that, alongside workplace reform and deeper obligation, the ones large mind-set modifications need to be supported by using ladies (particularly) quitting people suited at artwork. If you experience this, then you definately need to paintings on WHY you are people charming at artwork, and the establishments of being great rather than being assertive. Being your health warrior is critical while you are taking movement to ditching your human beings pleaser. You need a each day exercise which includes your Essential Me Time Maintenance, and a willpower to fierce love for yourself.

Let's move again to Marike. Being 'super', Marike didn't propose the ultra-cutting-edge piece of studies. What is the very last effects of that? This new piece of studies is probably uncovered via some other researcher who then receives the credit score rating. She might also stall in her profession. She may additionally additionally moreover feel disempowered, plenty much less than, inauthentic, and lacking in integrity. This will all have a knock-on effect on Marike's self guarantee. She will begin to doubt herself and keep herself once more. She have to get green with envy, and hundreds negativity have to breed from here.

How about 'assertive' Marike? She places forward the piece of new research. She has a few snarky behaviour to deal with from her group. Perhaps she receives the bloodless shoulder for a while. Not extremely good BUT what need to take region from right right here? She receives given a trendy mission to paintings on, or some other employer sees her work and hires her. Perhaps not some component splendid takes location but as an alternative she has possession over her perspectives, trusts her judgement, and feels extra confident. Maybe subsequent time Jo acquired't presume she may be great and could address her with more equality and admire. What Jo does or doesn't do isn't important. What Marike does and how she feels because of no longer people fascinating is what counts. From here on in, what you do and the way you experience due to no longer humans appealing is what topics.

We can not good deal the ripple effect as well. Let's say some one-of-a-kind ladies in Marike's crew sees what she has finished. They recognize Jo, too. OK, it's fair to count on there may be some bitchiness. But some women should check Marike and anticipate, 'Hell certain. She has stood in her strength. Maybe I have to do that too.'

So likely, instead of volunteering to organise the personnel Christmas do, and being the simplest doing the dishes or the only who laughs the entirety off, you are making a few choices to face more for your energy at artwork. You can however be a kind, thoughtful and supportive member at artwork with out disempowering yourself. Now, I am no longer pronouncing this could be easy. It received't. And there is probably some women who have deep internal misogyny (see financial disaster eleven) who will bitch about you at the back of your once more (or passive-aggressively internal earshot). Attitudes don't trade in a single day.

Let's take a look at any other situation – humans charming due to bitchy ladies at art work. Yes, the administrative center is, lamentably, notwithstanding the truth that a breeding floor for playground-fashion bitchiness.

Let me introduce you to Ayesha. She is proper at everything but in no way likes to reveal all and sundry else up. Ayesha is humorous, fantastic, multi-proficient, and a person who champions awesome women. She is also a people pleaser. She is effects popular however doesn't agree with in herself so is constantly self-deprecating, i.E. I'll positioned myself down in a greater humorous and sharp manner than you may. She's damn right at placing herself down and she or he's funny so human beings snigger collectively collectively along with her. People moreover pick out up consciously, or unconsciously, on how she comes across. 'Pushover.' 'Too awesome.' 'She'll in no way say no.' Can you comprehend any of this in you or to your relationships? And possibly, virtually perhaps, you realize the ones judgments which you, yourself, have made approximately other women. Oooh … that's a radical (and uncomfortable) sprinkle of self-popularity, proper there!

Ayesha manages a group of ladies in a charitable business corporation and he or she or he has presently been promoted. She is beginning to be aware that a number of her business enterprise are not contributing: their art work is lacklustre, their mind-set is terrible, and they are having a bad effect on their enterprise overall performance and morale. She isn't feeling confident approximately a way to method this – she doesn't need her organization to dislike her.

Reflection Point: Let's take a second right right here. This is your cue to prevent and suppose how frequently at art work you've been in situations in which you have got were given been involved approximately your group buddies disliking you. And sure, I am searching at YOU. How plenty electricity have you ever exhausted on this?

Newly promoted, Ayesha desires to take time to get to recognize her crew and the way wonderful to manipulate them. She conducts considerate one-to-ones in which she coaches every of them, installing vicinity motion plans and overview dates. This works with more than one them; it turns out they had been previously mismanaged and micro controlled. The interest and time Ayesha spends with them truely will pay off. However, with Hayley, it doesn't. She does the bare minimum and is now speaking to exceptional groups about how crap a supervisor Ayesha is.

Ayesha looks like she's once more at rectangular one – she consumes plenty electricity seeking out a way to deal with this. She talks over the scenario together together with her friends, going round in circles and now not developing with any answer that doesn't comprise Hayley not liking her. Well, she can also want to do now not anything, right? She should really maintain on looking for to assuage Hayley – but at what price?

Her organization's ordinary performance suffers

Their responsibilities need to war to move again collectively

Ayesha has a ton more art work and pressure

Most importantly, Ayesha's self assurance and belief in herself will weaken and, allow's be truly sincere here, Hayley isn't going to love or recognize her more. Instead, she'll maintain treating Ayesha with contempt, and this may rub off on excellent organization individuals and function long-term destructive effects. Ayesha wishes to perform a little element radical for her. She needs to no longer be notable.

Ayesha is aware of a few trouble desires to trade. She goes through the 7-Step Exploration, makes use of the resources to help her in remembering who she desires to be at artwork and, most importantly, makes a preference to now not human beings please. She listens to her instinct that is telling her to have an expert primarily based and brave verbal exchange with Hayley at artwork. Ayesha invitations Hayley to be sincere too, however units a tone of general professionalism. She involves a selection that Hayley doesn't want to love her however Ayesha does need to be dealt with with respect. She does it her manner, compassionately and with boundaries.

You are going to stand some resistance and in all likelihood some bitchiness at artwork.

The choice lies with you. Do you need to human beings please to try and make every person along with you or, and that could be a general cliché, be real to you and be guided via way of your values of compassion and courage? Ultimately, you haven't any control over special humans's evaluations and feelings. Trying to manipulate them is a shape of manipulation coming from an area of worry.

If you're guided by using your personal values, then extraordinary people may not consisting of you – however you could like you. At the save you of the day, as you're the most effective who has to spend time with your self every day, your very very own self-respect is lots greater important.

And I need to tell you that Ayesha did cope with Hayley in a compassionate manner, and Hayley determined to head away the group. Now Ayesha's group is a buzzing, supportive and a hit organization who've won awards of their region. Most crucially,

Ayesha feels she appreciates and respects herself at artwork, and doesn't enjoy the want to satisfaction.

Section 4: People fascinating in Business, Leadership and Your Purpose

Whether you have got have been given a corporation, endure in mind yourself a frontrunner, or recognize what your reason is (or now not), this segment is for you. If you have got a business enterprise organisation proper now, and need it to accumulate fulfillment, you want to upward push up close and private along aspect your human beings pleaser – otherwise, she can be capable of block your course and located a glass-ceiling for your achievement! Your corporation is an extension of you, your values, and the time and electricity you pour into it. If you're humans captivating for your commercial business enterprise, you're stunting your growth.

If you don't currently have your very own organization however plan to inside the destiny, the ideas I proportion on this section will assist prevent human beings proper troubles early on, and make beginning your employer a chunk plenty less painful.

Being a frontrunner in these instances requires entire authenticity and to expose up absolutely. Neither of those arise whilst your human beings pleaser is running the display. Being a leader seems and feels very first rate to big humans in a single-of-a-type situations, whether or now not that be critical due to the fact the parent you want to be, because the buddy you need to be, or through championing a task you need to begin up. People charming could have an effect on all styles of control and make the whole lot plenty more tough.

People suitable can save you the right clients/goal market/contacts from connecting with you. When you permit pass of being fine and diluting your message to make it extra palatable, or forestall weakening your limitations throughout the phrases of your business enterprise, for instance, functionality clients will enjoy your actual electricity and the whole lot will click into area.

We close to this phase (and ebook) collectively along with your reason – the holy grail of what we spend lots time as industrial corporation owners and leaders searching for. What your art work, manage, and enterprise company represents is an out of doors manifestation of your reason. Blocking this via human beings eye-catching is a waste of your innate provides, and a real disserve to you and the arena.

In this section, I'm going to percentage private reminiscences of being an entrepreneur for 10 years, having had a 6-figure commercial agency and received a couple of awards. While that sounds accurate (and I'm happy with my achievements), I'm most pleased with the instances I've carried out commercial enterprise enterprise my way, after I've lead with braveness and compassion, and after I've in reality embodied my reason. I want to percentage insights and techniques to assist you with ditching people attractive in your business enterprise so you, too, can hook up with your cause, and use your superpowers (presents) to be an powerful chief, now not definitely in business corporation, but in all areas of your life.

Chapter 13: The Five Superpowers

It feels superb to complete this ebook talking approximately the five Sensitive Superpowers. You have many, of route, however I want to spotlight the number one 5 that I use in my personal artwork, and with my community. They every play a significant element in how you want, stay, paintings, lead and join. I'm going to take you via each Superpower so you can get a revel in of the way, via manner of ditching your humans pleaser, you can use them to their fullest capability as you blaze the path on your business enterprise (and lifestyles).

I speak approximately Purpose, Platform and Privilege in my paintings. What I imply via those phrases are as follows:

Purpose: What you have got got were given are available in this earth to do and revel in. If, proper now, you're now not high-quality what this is, believe that your adventure to letting cross of your humans pleaser will take you nearer; all will unfold.

Platform: The small or large platform you have were given - whether that be social media and/or buddies, colleagues, clients and own family - wherein you could have an effect on with the resource of sharing your mind and mind.

Privilege: I are seeking recommendation from my privilege as my white pores and pores and pores and skin privilege - the societal advantages that I am afforded because I am white – and use it to expand marginalised voices to help the movement for social justice.

People proper may have an effect on every of these three subjects and the impact we desire to make. Leadership requires that we use our systems and privilege for the extra right and step completely into our purpose – very difficult even as your inner people pleaser is on foot the show!

By default of no longer humans appealing, you are being a leader in your art work (and lifestyles). Not conforming to social or family norms or pressure manner which you are forging a modern-day course. Sometimes you've got role fashions; every so often you don't. Creating that new course and taking walks it calls which will connect to 5 of your Sensitive Superpowers. These superpowers will serve and assist you – as long as you decide to ditching the want to delight.

COURAGE

What this superpower method for a getting higher humans pleaser:

The braveness to pay attention to what's important to you. The courage to now not do what a person else wishes you to do. The braveness to say no.

The assignment so as to paintings on: Learning how to mention no.

When I first commenced out off in self-employment as a contractor, I felt the want to mention sure to all customers, to all of the wishes, and to ensure anyone modified into happy. The concept of announcing no, of turning a patron away, or of not taking the wonderful I became provided changed into horrifying. What if the art work dried up? What if no cash came in? I ended up operating all-ingesting hours (in no way capable of transfer off), have turn out to be available 24/7 (hello, loss of barriers), and changed into beneath charging. Most importantly, I undervalued the paintings I even have emerge as doing. It come to be in particular arduous.

In my first business business enterprise, t.E.A.M, my commercial company partner and I had been so new to the sport. We had zero enterprise revel in and no coins within the again parents. We were surely building our commercial company on enthusiasm by myself, which we every had in abundance. We installation our training and workshops after which worked backwards, building the organisation spherical those services. One manager, who we had worked for in advance than, desired to put money into our schooling however saved haggling at the rate. She ended up paying the least for our services and modified into the maximum tough and traumatic of all our customers. We very quickly found out to employer up our limitations!

It grow to be lucky that I determined out this lesson so early on in my employer. I determined that pronouncing no to clients that did now not match or who tried to reduce my charges freed up time, strength and availability for customers who have been a miles higher healthful. It supposed being brave sufficient to mention no.

We didn't do a bargain greater training with that specific manager, but we did have the distance so that you can artwork with extraordinary managers who have been glad to pay our expenses and were a joy to art work with.

Customer organization and satisfaction in some thing your corporation or tasks offer is paramount – however does humans charming equal properly results? In a nutshell, no. Energy is critical. Even if we will't articulate 'that' feeling, we get a revel in of some factor being 'off' in our gut. Sometimes the vibe sincerely isn't proper. If we are feeling this, but nonetheless discover ourselves announcing positive to a few component that need to be a hard no, then we want to check in with our people pleaser.

Being brave enough to mention no to human beings is vital for your fulfillment in company; to displaying up because of the truth the leader you want to be, and to get toward your cause.

EMPATHY

What thIs superpower manner for a getting better humans pleaser:

To definitely revel in and method your very personal energy and emotions for readability and self perception. It is crucial which you apprehend what energy is yours, and what isn't.

Challenge a terrific manner to artwork on: How to preserve sturdy and wholesome limitations.

Being empathetic looks as if such a present to me in my company and control, and is a massive part of my purpose.

However, it took me numerous years to stand up to now. Throughout my industrial corporation, I've been a educate in severa guises. For a while, I had susceptible barriers inside my schooling durations, allowing people to off load the entirety onto me. So, I would possibly get exhausted or overwhelmed. An example is as quickly as I used to lead an in person membership organization for female marketers. I would possibly lead a workshop for the morning with a tea ruin half of way through. For the primary six months, I'd by no means have a damage, as that tea spoil could become with a person off-loading onto me. I'd run to the rest room moments in advance than the second one half of of started out and sense my power lagging. I desired to please sincerely absolutely everyone and be to be had for them to chat with me but it have become hard. I knew some difficulty had to shift. In this example, I set myself a boundary: I'd cease the primary 1/2, depart the distance, and cross again to start the second 1/2. I stuck with it. It felt lots higher for my strength and the general energy of the workshop. Consider it this manner – in case you want to help and help humans, you could most effective do that if you help and manual your self.

For you that could appear like:

Taking breaks whilst you're going for walks

Doing your exercise earlier than you begin artwork

Knowing the warning signs of crush and route correcting because of this

Stating your barriers - out loud, in writing, on social media, in patron contracts, in your net internet site - and following thru with them

If you say some aspect isn't proper, being prepared to stand with the aid of it

Empathy without kindness to yourself has a restrict, or becomes conditional upon others on your paintings. Empathy when you have labored to your people pleaser manner you are open and easy because of the truth you've got were given boundaries. This is in which you step up as a pacesetter and turn out to be the conduit for change.

COMPASSION (IN ACTION)

What this superpower approach for a recuperating human beings pleaser:

It technique embodying your values and expressing them without worry of what someone may think. It way being organized to be judged and to be visible. Your people pleaser will attempt to prevent you from being harm this manner, however your embodiment and devotion manner greater than whether or not some people which includes you or now not.

Challenge that allows you to paintings on: Taking the movement irrespective of what others expect because of the truth you apprehend it's miles in alignment with you.

Compassion with out motion is lip company. Within your employer, management, and connecting together together with your motive, compassion in movement way you're mission real existence.

Only you can decide your visibility inside any vicinity of your existence. If you're invested for your paintings - whether or not or not that be a component hustle, your personal business organization, or a project - shrinking to be greater palatable or an awful lot plenty less threatening to others will do you and your enterprise a huge disservice. You need to experience your whole being in all of your artwork and those want to look and sense you. 'Don't get too massive for your boots,' , 'Who does she count on she is,' and lots of others. Are all constraints designed to preserve you small and towing the road.

Take a moment now to take in the ones phrases: you need to get comfortable with the concept that you are going to piss a person off, that your art work isn't for all people, and that you'll probable shine a chunk too colourful for some people.

With the arrival of social media, society has become lots greater transparent in plenty of techniques, not usually in phrases of fact, however in how visible everyone are. Very little is off limits in recent times, from what humans are consuming for breakfast, to their preferred Netflix shows, to the passive-competitive arguments they're having. With your artwork, you will be on social media in some way and with that comes judgement. You can also have heard it said that human beings are too busy thinking about themselves and their non-public lives to be judging you. It's now not actual. People pick out. They will decide some thing you're announcing or do, or don't say or do. You'll be judged for being vocal. You'll be judged in your silence. Make no mistake – you will be judged. Therefore, it saves pretty a while and heartache so you can do your art work the manner you want to and, as many a well-known music may want to say, permit the haters hate! You can not please all and sundry, and neither is it your venture to, so why not stay with captivating your self together with your artwork. Mistakes are a part of having your private business (and surely a part of being alive), and if your worry of being judged stems from perfectionism, you have got were given it in you to permit that flow.

I've had humans tell me they judged me – I've spoken in the front of big audiences, been the visitor blogger in awesome regions, and written about my reviews of being abused. None of these reviews felt cushty, however they may be no longer supposed to. Sometimes, I've felt mainly anxious however the choice to completely expand and be present in my artwork has been a splendid deal large than the priority of different people judging me.

This superpower has to go back from a place of deep compassion for your self and others this is cultivated thru your imperfect workout.

What this superpower method for a convalescing people pleaser:

The capacity to recognize what your creativity appears and seems like. To specific your self creatively.

Challenge on the way to paintings on: Discover what creativity way for you and go along with it without looking beforehand to validation.

When you are human beings appropriate, you're disconnected collectively with your Higher Self. You also are disconnected together with your creativity. You might be relying on others to offer you thoughts, or not shifting forward until your concept has been confirmed with the approval of others.

I've had the delight of operating with pretty quite a variety of girls who've had exceptional obligations/companies/thoughts. A tremendous proportion struggled with others' perceptions of who they 'ought to' be in their agency, how plenty they 'ought to' fee for tasks, and the way confident or no longer they 'must' be. Success – anything which means, feels or looks as if to you - can handiest be accessed through your creative expression.

Writing a ebook about people stunning as a getting better human beings pleaser has been a amazing exploration of what present day expression in truth technique to me. I want this ebook to be treasured to you. I furthermore don't want to put in writing what I am 'expected' to install writing, or to conform to what a traditional self-assist ebook can also moreover seem like. I've observed my intuitive steerage as soon as I revel in a few component desires to be said. I've shared from my coronary heart and expressed myself in the way that is my reality proper now. This form of creativity connects and creates in a way that is a whole lot more powerful than conforming to a few difficulty self-help elegant is presently famous. How I particular myself in six months, one year, and five years from now might be special. Right now, it topics to me that I am real in my cutting-edge expression on this 2d. This has been made viable due to the reality I'm not concerned approximately what others expect.

INTUITION

What this superpower manner for a enhancing people pleaser:

Being guided thru your intuition, no longer out of your ego, allowing you to make outstanding business organization choices. You pay hobby on your internal voice, not the critics.

Your project to work on: Tuning out the outdoor noise so you will pay attention your instinct.

I vividly consider a communication with my mum. I was on a educate and had known as her. It become at the peak of t.E.A.M's fulfillment and I turned into excited to allow Mum understand approximately the awards we were nominated for. She listened to me, congratulated me, and then said, 'But you don't need to get too a success now.' I'll permit that sink in for a 2nd. I certainly cannot recollect what I said in reaction but the reminiscence stayed with me. It surfaced all all over again not that extended within the beyond as soon as I emerge as operating on a few beliefs I had round cash and success. There were a few limitations I had faced, and the idea of not getting 'too massive in your boots' is one that I'd heard so frequently when I become younger. These varieties of testimonies disconnect you from your intuition.

I realised that human beings attractive isn't just about my experience, however moreover approximately modelling a strong empowered presence for my little one and breaking generations of playing small, trying to meet expectancies, and now not paying attention to intuitive guidance. My mum had a robust revolutionary and entrepreneurial streak, my grandma too – it changed into possibly referred to as 'contemporary' in her era. However, it emerge as most effective allowed to a extremely good aspect. They have been both quite intuitive however in no manner completely trusted their instinct. My grandma had extraordinary psychic gadgets however didn't recollect in herself sufficient to apply them. My mum had brilliant recuperation skills but could in no way permit herself to truly heal so you can absolutely encompass the ones talents. I'm proper right here breaking all of the cycles. I didn't have a look at any rulebook to start my private enterprise employer, and I didn't wait for clearly each person's permission to be a mamma and an entrepreneur. I'm proudly owning my psychic gives and my recuperation competencies. However, it took steady reputation of these inherently ingrained generational tales to enhance my obstacles. It took willpower to my intuition.

Have you fallen into the hole of seeking to please others in advance than your self on your business agency or as a frontrunner? Perhaps it's been because of fear of judgement, or playing small to healthy an expectation someone else has of you? It's time to blast via those poisonous memories and step in reality into the opportunity and potential of your artwork.

Our voices may be heard in a completely new manner. What a privilege it is a very good way to proportion, assist to inform, and signpost for the great unique! As leaders, we can construct deeper connections, foster empathy, and amplify what isn't always being heard.

We have been blessed to be born into the ones in particular hard instances with get proper of entry to to aid and connection like no exceptional. The net has made the arena and organization greater reachable, connecting us to property, opportunities, people, and limitless opportunities that our mothers and grandmothers didn't have. Let us not blow this opportunity through human beings stunning. What a waste of your items that might be.

There is not any time to waste. Your human beings and the area need you. They want you without a doubt to your electricity, remembering who you're – faraway from humans charming. The techniques you could help, the ideas that you have, the motives that want your assist, the voices you need to extend, and your God given motive all call for that you allow go of the need to delight and be 'amazing', and completely embody your devices.

A word on cause: How do I comprehend what my reason is?

If you don't enjoy like what your motive is, you're not on my own. We can become so fixated (and frustrated) on finding our motive but in case you don't however recognize what it's far, that's OK. Honestly. I can guarantee you which you're at the proper course, right now.

Some people may additionally furthermore say, 'My motive is to experience delight,' even as others are searching out nirvana. For a few, it's approximately being at One; for others, it's feeling fulfilled. As our ego performs this type of massive detail in our enjoy of existence, my real primary tip for connecting along with your reason is to make connecting with the prevailing second a top precedence even though the prevailing 2nd feels particularly uncomfortable and hard. It can be considered that we've got got an inner and an outer motive – your internal purpose associated with connection for your Highest Self/Source, and your outer in your contribution collectively together with your affords within the global.

Connecting collectively along side your superpowers will deliver you closer to your internal and outer purpose. Each of the superpowers I clearly have shared on this phase help to attach you in a deep way. Here's how:

Courage: to get admission to your courage, assemble it like a muscle and exercise it manner you're coming nearer and in the route of your reason. You can't exercising courage and now not be permitting area in your cause to go returned through.

Empathy: as a sensitive, your empathy is innate. When you are linked in your empathy in an empowered way (with barriers and deep attention), you pave the manner in your motive to come decrease again thru you.

Compassion (in Action): on every occasion you're taking movement primarily based mostly on an problem that is crucial to you, e.G. Some factor that you cannot stay silent on, you're moving into your motive. Each time you pay attention some thing and it movements you, and you revel in referred to as to speak up approximately it, you're moving into your purpose.

Creativity: your creativity is part of your soul's expression, but that appears for you. Each time you tap into your creativity, you're tapping into your soul's expression and welcoming your reason to transport internal and out of you.

Intuition: that is your innate understanding and is inextricably related together together together with your purpose. Your soul's whispers come through your intuition and bring you together collectively with your motive. Stay close to your intuition – your motive is there.

Chapter 14: Psychology Of Assertiveness

Assertiveness isn't what you do, it's far who you're! –Shakti Gawain

Being assertive will alternate your life. If you're capable to speak what you want while nonetheless respecting the critiques of others, then you definitely without a doubt're much more likely to get your desires met. It closes the door on confusion; the ones spherical you won't surprise what you expect of them. They'll already understand because you made your wishes, desires, similarly in your obstacles smooth.

In this financial ruin, I am going to take a deep dive into the psychology of status up for your self. Why does assertiveness come so without issues for a few while others want to installation masses of try to beautify this potential? Why is saying no seen in this kind of terrible light? What's the difference between being assertive and aggressive? These are a number of the questions we'll explore inside the segment under. What's more, I'll additionally share with you what you'll advantage if you method lifestyles in a self-confident manner.

What Does It Mean to Be Assertive?

Each character seeks their non-public very last results in existence. When your desires warfare with those of some different, assertiveness can be one of the identifying elements in whether or not or now not matters will flip out your manner or not. How assertive you're will decide how difficult you push to get what you need (Ames, 2008).

When you're pretty assertive, you gained't shy away from attempting to steer others to see your side. You moreover received't be afraid to shield your desires. However, one crucial issue to don't forget is that assertive conduct does no longer disregard others' rights or emotions (Speed, Goldstein & Goldfried, 2017). It's about speakme your desires without making desires of numerous people or lashing out at the same time as your desires aren't met. When recognize is lacking, you're now not being assertive; you're being rude, and that's no longer a great trait to have. It doesn't take masses to be categorized as a 'whinge' at the same time as you're a girl and, opposite to popular notion, that doesn't give you strength, but takes it away. Your pals might be a great deal less open closer to you, they'll be more protecting, and this could near many doors that could've delivered approximately fantastic possibilities.

That doesn't advise being overly assertive is an absolute no-no. At instances, it can be a need. I apprehend it looks as if I am contradicting myself, however take into account your assertiveness as having an depth dial. When your little one has low arrogance and also you find out that they lied approximately finishing their homework, you'll most effective turn the dial to just above low whilst you difficulty them. On the alternative hand, while you're a primary responder on the scene of an twist of destiny and lives are at stake, assertiveness is crucial, so you'll crank the dial as a whole lot as max.

Reading the scenario and crowd is the whole lot in phrases of being assertive. It can be hard as we navigate a large fashion of conditions each day, however you'll want to learn how to use a aggregate of strategies. Too plenty or too little assertiveness and neither you nor the alternative character gets what you preference for. In the stop, your purpose need to be to upward thrust up for what you need at the identical time as trying to gain an agreeable very last effects for all. Yet, I don't want you to assume which you'll generally be able to decide an answer this is useful to all people. Unfortunately, that isn't how life works, however you need to be thrilled with looking to accommodate others' need and desires whilst seeking to get yours met.

It comes all of the manner all the way down to interpersonal assertiveness. Yet how assertive we're in any given second is based totally totally on our motivation, expectancies, and disasters of self-law (Ames, Lee & Wazlawek, 2017). This manner that it could be tough within the beginning to unblur the line among being competitive, passive-competitive, and assertive, but because the region says, "Practice makes great!" Passivity is by no means the solution. It is your life we're talking about right proper right here and also you satisfactory get one threat to live it. There's no time to take a seat down once more and permit others manage it due to the reality you're too terrified of coming across as aggressive.

In time, assertiveness becomes a dependancy and distinguishing it from aggression will be 2nd nature. So, don't be tough on yourself as you learn how to gently, and with out disgrace, ask for what you want.

Also, it's easy for girls to experience egocentric after they positioned their desires first. When you start to paintings on growing more confident, it will get less complicated and much less complicated to brush aside this untruth. As you mature on your assertiveness, you'll understand that asking and combating for what you need isn't self-centered—it's a shape of self-care and also you deserve it.

The Benefits of Being Assertive

Assertiveness comes with many blessings. Not only does it prevent special people from the use of you as a doormat, however it moreover prevents you from on foot over others.

If you question me, the impact assertiveness has on intellectual fitness, relationships, and undertaking satisfaction hasn't been given the attention it deserves. I'm stunned through what number of humans, specifically ladies, on this issue in time despite the fact that lack assertiveness and the way this influences their careers and lives negatively. One have a have a look at determined that assertiveness combats anxiety, stress, and despair in high faculty university college students (Eslami et al., 2016) and every other discusses how assertiveness might also moreover even help you triumph over social tension (Smith, 1975). I can guarantee you that the perks of living extra assertively are far-attaining—it changed all components of my lifestyles. Here are some examples of what quality subjects you could expect while you arise for yourself.

Self-esteem improve: There's not anything higher for your conceitedness than taking duty on your life and speaking up for your self. How you notice your self is basically based mostly on the reaction you get from the ones round you, and how you act will effect how others see you. In exclusive phrases, if you behave in a manner that represents low arrogance, then that is what human beings will respond to, and that is what you can come to be believing about yourself. On the possibility hand, if you assert yourself, humans will deal with you with extra appreciate and at the way to increase yourself assurance. Confident human beings are perceived as smart, succesful, and as higher leaders. Those are some individual developments a exceptional way to take you places!

Become extra green: When you look at to say 'No,' you'll have extra time to spend on property you need to and now not have to. You won't revel in compelled to provide a while to trivial matters but can cognizance on critical responsibilities as an alternative. It's interesting to word that you may say no with out using the word. We'll cover this in extra detail in a later monetary disaster.

Experience normal fulfillment: People who're too passive generally tend to sacrifice lots to make others satisfied. This takes place in all elements in their existence. Even deciding on a restaurant for dinner is left within the hands of a person else. Although you might imagine that is noble, it will handiest motive frustration while you continually permit surely every body else get subjects their manner. When you're assertive, you acquired't be afraid to talk up and say, "I'm in the temper for Chinese this night." You recognize what? The character who offers a proposal generally in the long run ends up getting what they want due to the reality the opportunity human beings are too afraid to speak up. Where to eat may moreover sound like an inconsequential instance, but if you can learn how to percentage your opinion in such small conditions, elevating your voice on more vital problems turns into much less complicated. Soon you'll get what you want—in a few thing massive or small manner.

Better preference-making talents: When you're assertive, your choices aren't so emotionally driven. You're capable of take a extra independent stance in which you may weigh the specialists and cons and make an knowledgeable preference. Aggressive humans, on the other hand, have a propensity to be confrontational in their choice-making, which means that it's far driven via emotion and no longer good judgment.

Be taken critically: People don't take you seriously if you exchange your opinion in an attempt to come across as extra agreeable. Even worse, they will take benefit of you after they comprehend you're so with out troubles swayed. However, while you're assured for your angle and upward push up for what you recollect in, humans will admire your limitations. They will understand that your 'no' isn't any.

To enjoy the above, you need to observe even as to be assertive and the manner assertive you need to be. If we're speaking about a social setting, immoderate assertiveness can harm relationships (Ames & Flynn, 2007). On the turn element, low assertiveness in a piece putting may additionally moreover cause low success.

Still, regardless of the depth, assertiveness is a combination of honesty and apprehend. You're honest about targets and desires, however you admire that unique human beings aren't liable for making them a truth.

The Case Against Being Assertive

There are women who determine now not to say themselves. Usually, this choice is pushed by using fear. Other instances, it's far because of the fact they query their nicely definitely really worth. Whatever their cause can be, there's no legitimate purpose for no longer being assertive.

Below I will percentage with you a number of the most commonplace reasons why girls decide in competition to speakme up.

People receives indignant at me.

This is completely primarily based mostly on fear of retaliation or rejection. The teach of perception goes some thing like this: "If I'm assertive, X gets mad because I'm making it hard for them to do things their manner. When people get mad, awful topics typically take area. So, allow's now not make human beings mad."

Pushing your want and dreams aside due to the reality you're fearful of how humans will react may also do away with a few soreness within the advocate time, but in the end, it's going to cause frustration, anger, and resentment.

People will revel in harm.

Guilt is the using pressure behind this way of questioning. It stems from the belief that during case you get your way, someone else isn't getting theirs. Throughout this ebook, I've referred to that proper assertiveness is doing all of your excellent to provide you a win-win answer. If that isn't possible, there's although no reason if you want to believe that someone will enjoy horrible or crumble due to the fact you voiced your opinion and matters occurred to show out for your pick out.

You shouldn't lose sleep in case you assert your self in a deferential manner. There's no longer something devious approximately assertiveness—no individual is conniving with all people to make sure they get their way. Assertiveness is ready talking overtly and definitely and letting matters take their direction.

People received't like me.

It have turn out to be pretty a rude awakening at the same time as the notion hit me that not everyone I meet will like me.

In many times, I obtained't even want to do or say some issue; they received't like how I do my hair, comply with my makeup, the garments I placed on, and lots of others. But you recognize what? That's ok! I don't like everyone I meet both. It's human. Knowing this, it's less hard to get over the concern that people will prevent liking you at the same time as you're assertive. Sharing your opinion isn't always nagging. Asking for a few component is not disturbing. If a person reports it that manner, it isn't your problem. Remember what you have a look at earlier: what human beings keep in mind you isn't your company.

I can almost guarantee you that assertiveness completed right won't purpose human beings to dislike you. It is even as you're competitive or passive-aggressive that they'll be a whole lot much less than stimulated. You'll examine all about the versions a chunk in some time.

If you don't have something remarkable to mention…

My mom taught me to maintain quiet when I didn't have anything amazing to mention. I'm sure you had been told the identical or some aspect comparable. When it comes to assertiveness, this advice doesn't follow in any respect. Why? Because being assertive isn't about being nasty or insulting; it's miles going hand in hand with recognize.

When you're assertive, you don't permit things building up until you explode and growth the threat of announcing some thing you would possibly regret. Instead, you seize troubles after they rise up and deal with them in a relaxed and collected manner.

It's no biggie.

These phrases used to transport my lips on a every day basis earlier than I discovered to be more assertive. I take into account the internal feeling that would go together with it. It was a mixture of worry, embarrassment, and self-deprecation. I didn't revel in worth sufficient to say "No, I don't agree," and might go with a few issue modified into counseled. No biggie, right? Wrong!

Minimizing your very very own need and desires, and not honoring your barriers to cope with others', isn't always a wholesome technique to lifestyles. It will only feed into the idea that you're lots a whole lot less-than and could do nothing on your self-esteem.

Catch your self in advance than you are pronouncing some thing that pushes your desires, values, or critiques to the issue. You have a right to upward thrust up for what you want.

People already apprehend what I need.

It is probably wonderful if human beings had been psychic, but sadly, they're most probable not. You can't count on human beings to are looking forward to what you need or the way you feel. You're placing your self up for unhappiness if you think others recognize what goes through your thoughts. It furthermore comes throughout as extraordinarily narcissistic if you expect a person must just realise what to do to make you glad.

Instead of staying quiet and hoping someone will guess what you want, inform them. Be direct on the identical time as you percentage your expectations. There's a far better hazard you'll get what you need if there's no ambiguity and anybody is at the equal net net web page.

That covers some well-known motives why ladies can also determine against being assertive. Nevertheless, I think it's far crucial to have a take a look at why jogging ladies fail to talk up, disagree, negotiate, or advocate themselves. See if any points within the following segment relate to you.

Advocating for Yourself inside the Workplace

Many ladies take shipping of as real with that the place of work runs on gain: you do proper artwork and you get rewarded. The fact is that top art work is not all it takes. If you need to get in advance, you've got to reveal them which you're assured in your competencies. One way to do this is to be assertive.

Regrettably, ladies commonly have a tendency to keep away from doing the matters with a view to help them raise of their careers. Let's look at the four biggest fears referring to assertiveness that keep women from accomplishing their capacity in the administrative center.

1. Concern over speakme assertively

Women frequently melt their speech. Instead of the use of strength phrases, we use weaker language. We normally have a tendency to frame our sentences spherical

"I assume" or "I enjoy." Assertive human beings, as an opportunity, don't predicate what they are saying—they arrive right out and say it without softening or qualifying it!

"I suppose that could be a awesome idea" will become "This is a high-quality concept." Similarly, "I sense that is the right issue to do" becomes "This is what we want to do."

There's hundreds greater conviction in the latter, extra assertive examples, right?

We've hooked up that assertiveness desires to be tailored counting on the state of affairs. The same is actual within the administrative center. There may be times even as softening your language isn't only suitable however crucial. For instance, you may try this at the same time as the time entails treatment a war. This is whilst "I anticipate" and "I enjoy" statements may go notable. But if you're having a extreme assembly collectively along side your organization members, it's excellent to step proper right into a extra self-confident and assured position if you want them to peer you as a leader. This doesn't offer you with permission to be condescending, impolite, or belittling even though, so watch your tone.

2. Fear of negotiating

There is a large profits hole amongst males and females. Not exceptional do girls earn substantially much less than their male counterparts do, however we additionally typically tend to fee less. It's scary at the same time as you do the arithmetic. A $5,000 difference in your first undertaking translates to a huge lack of $ hundred,000 over the span of your profession.

Are you a person who thinks there may be nothing more awkward than soliciting for a enhance? It's as though we're programmed to revel in responsible about requesting money. There's moreover an element of no longer statistics our properly well worth, so we take what they offer because of the reality we assume that's the superb we will get or deserve. This want to come to an stop.

Women should begin being honest with themselves approximately their capabilities and what they may provide a agency. We had to get the equal qualification as our male opposite numbers to be eligible for a selected characteristic, so why don't we deserve similar repayment?

You need to take delivery of you're an asset to any enterprise agency and discover ways to negotiate for the income you deserve. No one else is going to do it for you.

When I have been given presented the position of Vice President I knew the compensation furnished modified into low. I didn't fault the guys making the provide due to the fact I apprehend businesses are seeking to do subjects as cheaply as feasible. Instead, I equipped myself with as plenty information as I probably may additionally want to, which includes cutting-edge worker salaries, employee retention, and comparative salaries at special companies. I supplied this information to them and I left that assembly with a proposal that become 20% better than the preliminary offer, plus retention and common overall performance-primarily based totally completely bonuses. I actually have by no means left a assembly feeling so empowered.

So, ask for what you're genuinely nicely worth. If you don't get it, the sensation of status up for your self will do away with some of the edge of disappointment.

three. Worry over inflicting warfare

Women excel at constructing and retaining relationships (Harvard Business Review, 2013). This is a precious information to have in existence and is a key component of fulfillment in a company surroundings. For this cause, we don't need to jeopardize our relationships with coworkers via standing up for ourselves. There's a trouble that assertive behavior may also moreover disenchanted others and probable result in conflict. People don't comprehend that war doesn't want to be a horrible revel in. When you use respectful language and stay goal, struggle can be enlightening. You'll quickly analyze that it is absolutely viable to be assertive without alienating every body—as long as you do it right.

You additionally must keep in mind which you aren't at artwork to make buddies. It's tremendous if you grow to be close at the side of your coworkers, but ultimately, you're there to art work and get the task completed. It's as a good deal as you to discover the right balance between growing a harmonious workplace and being assertive.

four. Dislike of self-promoting

Have you ever discovered how guys continuously boast about their achievements? It doesn't rely if you're popularity round a cocktail desk at a piece function or looking ahead to the red meat to grill at a network barbeque; they'll have some element to brag about. This is one of the motives why guys climb the enterprise ladder quicker than women.

As I stated earlier, suitable art work is not all it takes. People want to apprehend who you're, what you're capable of, and what cost you can convey to them. You need to sell your self. If those round you don't understand about your skills or your successes, why might they offer you an possibility?

I simply have a list of all my accomplishments and I'm not afraid to percentage it once I want to. I suppose even as human beings think about self-vending, they imagine someone obnoxiously bragging about themselves at the wrong time and area, inflicting everyone around them to sense uncomfortable. Don't worry, that's no longer the kind of self-selling I'm talking approximately. No one is going to invite you to percent your achievements at random moments and within the wrong putting.

However, whilst you're in a assembly at the side of your advanced discussing your future in the business enterprise, now not something should save you you from sharing your successes, thoughts, and contributions. Similarly, networking activities aren't the time and region to keep quiet approximately your qualifications and competencies both.

Consider growing a list of all of your achievements and reading over it periodically. Keeping the ones achievements at the forefront of your mind might also moreover even act as a hint self assure increase whenever you begin to doubt your abilities.

Spot the Difference: Assertive or Aggressive?

In psychology, assertiveness is described as a direct, corporation, notable movement alleged to sell equality in character-to-person relationships (Alberti & Emmons, 2008). That is vastly exceptional from what most humans understand it to be. The reality is, equity plays a key position in assertiveness. Assertiveness isn't always about manipulating someone into presenting you with what you want.

Psychologists Vagos and Pereira upload any other layer at the same time as defining assertiveness. They classify it as a "sturdy and one of a kind individual function through way of which healthy and horrible women and men may be distinguished" (2016). That is in which the primary distinction lies among assertiveness and bad behaviors which includes aggression, defensiveness, and rudeness.

To begin with, aggression has little regard for the rights of others. When you're assertive, you rise up on your rights with out infringing at the rights of others. In certainly one of a type terms, you need to be on same footing with the ones round you. Aggressive people, however, are most effective involved with themselves.

It's smooth that assertiveness is a prosocial conduct; aggression, no longer masses.

There are a few who keep in mind aggression as a subset of assertiveness and now not a conduct on its very very own (Ames, Lee & Wazlawek, 2017). Instead of being taken into consideration competitive, one may be labeled "over-assertive," or "aggressively assertive" (Thompson & Berenbaum, 2011). However, it doesn't depend what you call it, aggression now not often leads to success. You're much more likely to be ostracized than get a person to understand your opinion.

What approximately passive-aggression?

Well, allow's destroy it down. When you're passive, you supply in to what those spherical you want, and even as you're competitive, you best consider your non-public desires. So, being assertive can be considered a healthy medium.

Three Models of Assertiveness

There's no denying that assertiveness is complicated and closely impacted through someone's mind, feelings, and ideals.

Given the significance of assertiveness, many psychologists take a look at it and try to draw up models to offer an explanation for what it is and the way it works.

There are three fashions I'd like to percentage with you in essential terms due to the truth I maintain in thoughts they cover important factors which have an effect on how assertive a person is.

1. Forecasting Model

Many those who lack emotional recognition will assemble highbrow models of assertiveness. This is in which someone will visualize an very last outcomes primarily based on their stage of self-assuredness. So, earlier than they act, they believe the final outcomes and adapt how hard they push based totally mostly on the effects they expect. For instance:

If I am very assertive, I may also moreover get to persuade the group.

If I am passive, I may be visible as incapable of major and will emerge as getting walked over.

Forecasting can circulate both manner; it is able to be accurate, however additionally can be misleading.

We ought to recollect that the proper level of assertiveness relies upon at the character, the situation, and the fulfillment rate of past situations. In other terms, in case you're not used to repute up for your self, you're much more likely to forecast a negative very last effects inside the scenario in that you behave quite assertively.

2. Leadership Model

Brilliant leaders generally generally tend to very own a balance of developments and attributes (Zaccaro, 2007). This trait-based mind-set of management shifts the focus faraway from an growth of person functions and personalities. It indicates that talented leaders are solid and ordinary no matter the occasions. Furthermore, the control version of assertiveness shows that authentic leaders can distinguish among assertiveness and aggression, and they normally choose out the preceding.

3. Purposeful Conservation Model

According to Simon Black, there are four styles of responses on the assertiveness scale. Assertive and responsive are taken into consideration effective behavior, whereas competitive and passive are visible as self-defeating conduct (Black, 2017).

When you adopt an assertive or responsive mind-set, you're capable of successfully have an effect on others. Effective behavior is as smooth as sharing records or answering questions in a clean way, backing up your answers with actual elements and motives, or asking questions.

On the turn issue, sarcasm, placing yourself down, being condescending, and avoidance are self-defeating behaviors that harm relationships.

Positive behavior conserves the relationship we've got with the humans around us.

Learning to Be Assertive

Assertiveness education has grown through the years. One have a examine observed that monthly ninety-minute assertiveness training periods notably expanded assertiveness in nurses (Nakamura, 2017). In those schooling, the nurses would get a lecture on assertiveness followed with the useful resource of a roleplaying session. The take a look at observed that practising being assertive have turn out to be key in growing this capability. So, as you read thru this ebook, enjoy free to exercising on a friend or member of the family as often as crucial. But in advance than you do, make sure you understand the difference among assertiveness and aggression to avoid any tough emotions.

Vagos and Pereira proposed a cognitive-primarily based version of assertiveness (Vagos & Pereira, 2016). They suggest the subsequent steps for studying to be assertive:

Distinguish among assertiveness and aggression.

Learn to apprehend perceptions and feelings that result in aggression.

Understand a way to change the ones elements to inspire assertiveness and no longer aggression.

Let's have a examine a real-international instance.

You show up at artwork and greet your coworkers enthusiastically. One of them reacts rudely for your greeting and also you reply with anger.

When the difference amongst aggression and assertiveness, you'll be able to exchange the way you consider the situation. A greater assertive mind-set will give you the functionality to have a take a look at what came about with commonplace experience and plenty less emotion.

You'll endure in thoughts that your coworker's infant is decreasing teeth and now Mommy isn't getting tons sleep. This is the motive within the lower back of her impoliteness. So, rather than responding with aggression, you provide her a cup of espresso and ask if you could assist her with some thing. That assertive behavior shows her and your other coworkers that you are on pinnacle of things of your feelings and also you're capable of empathy.

With that being said, before we pass immediately to financial ruin , I need to percentage with you my top five recommendations on a way to be more assertive at art work due to the fact the functionality to voice your opinion and concerns, advocate for yourself, and negotiate is important in a employer placing in case you need to get everywhere. Of route, the ones suggestions are with out issues implemented to assertiveness in enormous, so don't skip earlier if you're not a career female!

www.ingramcontent.com/pod-product-compliance
Lightning Source LLC
Chambersburg PA
CBHW070735020526
44118CB00035B/1355